TEACHING in the Digital Age

SECOND EDITION

To my daughters Lauren and Grace
May your lives be a joyful and an exciting adventure as you grow up in the digital age and experience a world that will whet your appetite for what is possible through the powerful combination of understanding and technology. A wonderful journey lies ahead for your unique souls. Godspeed, my children.

Kristen J. Nelson

TEACHING in the Digital Age

Using the Internet to Increase Student Engagement and Understanding

SECOND EDITION

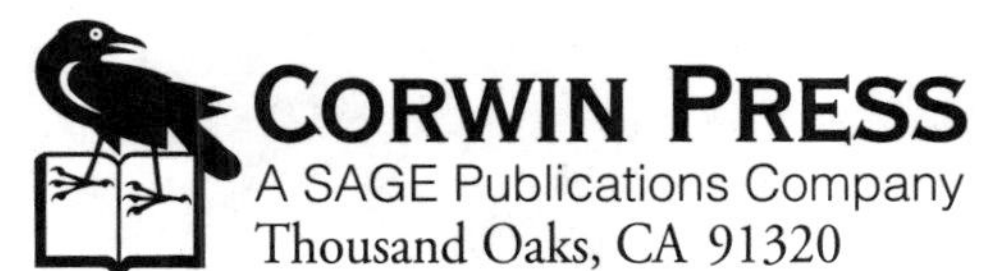

For information:

Corwin Press
A Sage Publications Company
2455 Teller Road
Thousand Oaks, California 91320
www.corwinpress.com

Sage Publications India Pvt. Ltd.
B 1/I 1 Mohan Cooperative Industrial Area
Mathura Road, New Delhi 110 044
India

Sage Publications Ltd.
1 Oliver's Yard
55 City Road
London EC1Y 1SP
United Kingdom

Sage Publications Asia-Pacific Pte. Ltd.
33 Pekin Street #02–01
Far East Square
Singapore 048763

Printed in the United States of America.

Library of Congress Cataloging-in-Publication Data

Nelson, Kristen J.
Teaching in the digital age: using the internet to increase student engagement and understanding/Kristen J. Nelson.—2nd ed.
p. cm.
Includes bibliographical references and index.
ISBN 978-1-4129-5565-2 (cloth)
ISBN 978-1-4129-5566-9 (pbk.)
1. Internet in education. 2. Multiple intelligences. I. Title.

LB1044.87.N452 2008
371.33'44678—dc22 2007011192

This book is printed on acid-free paper.

07 08 09 10 11 10 9 8 7 6 5 4 3 2 1

Acquisitions Editor: Hudson Perigo
Editorial Assistant: Jordan Barbakow
Production Editor: Veronica Stapleton
Copy Editor: Renee Willers
Typesetter: C&M Digitals (P) Ltd.
Proofreader: Ellen Brink
Indexer: Michael Ferreira
Cover Designer: Monique Hahn

Contents

Preface

During the 1990s, I, as most teachers, struggled with finding my own voice in a classroom full of rules, frameworks, standardized test scores, administrative expectations, and parents knocking on the door wondering what will happen to their precious bundles who do not turn in homework. I have been on a journey—a long odyssey of finding my own truth in this exciting, exhausting, and exhilarating profession called teaching.

During 18 years in education, I have learned that my responsibilities include recognizing students' individualities and unique styles, their backgrounds and current life circumstances, and their natural interests and motivations. When I began seeing students as distinct and special individuals, I was able to use all my knowledge, instructional tools, and strategies to help them become engaged and excited lifelong learners. I realized that one student's road map for learning is not identical to any other's, and my job is to provide experiences that engage students through their different intelligences, to appeal to their interests and motivations, and to support different rates of instruction.

After many years of teaching, my tool kit was full of theories, ideas, brain research findings, strategies, and instructional tools. Two of the most powerful tools that affected my teaching were the multiple intelligences theory and the Internet. At first glance, these two seem like an odd couple; yet, they can be integrated into the curriculum in the hands of a skilled teacher and can work together seamlessly to increase learning and understanding.

A friend who recently visited his child's classroom told me that it reminded him of his own sixth grade classroom. Thirty-three years had passed and yet the similarities were striking. As he got up to leave, he turned and said, "Can you imagine if you walked into an operating room 33 years ago and then saw one today and it was exactly the same? How depressing." I was bothered by the entire conversation. How could classrooms remain much the same when the world was changing at such a fast pace, when words such as *global economy*, *high tech*, and *.com* were ubiquitous in the mass media, and when brain research had shed so much light on how students' minds work?

Teaching in the Digital Age: Using the Internet to Increase Student Engagement and Understanding, Second Edition strives to provide a vision of how teaching and learning can be strengthened by technology combined with multiple intelligences and brain research. This book integrates the Internet, the theory of multiple intelligences, and brain research to help teachers design projects and activities that help students gain a deeper understanding of the curriculum. My goal is to provide educators with practical, yet research-based, material on how to use the Internet to increase student engagement and understanding. Many recent books provide sample stand-alone Internet activities and also offer visions of the potential the Internet brings into the classroom. Now that the Internet is used in the majority of K–12 classrooms throughout the United States, the main question has become, Is the Internet helping students learn what students need and want to learn?

Teaching in the Digital Age: Using the Internet to Increase Student Engagement and Understanding, Second Edition provides a framework for how Internet-based activities can blend the theory of multiple intelligences and brain research to help students learn and understand critical concepts and skills. As teachers learn to design lessons based on curriculum standards and strong assessments while using the Internet to provide engaging and challenging learning activities, students become empowered to learn and grow in new and exciting ways. I hope this book will provide a roadmap for teachers to become more familiar with the Internet, brain research, and the theory of multiple intelligences, and for them to see how these different tools can work together to strengthen teaching and learning.

This book represents one educator's effort to connect the dots of educational theory, instructional practice, and brain-based research with the hope of equipping teachers to walk into their classrooms each morning armed with the latest knowledge and research. I hope that classrooms of this century will take on a new look and feel as students are empowered through this type of informed and strategic teaching.

KRISTEN J. NELSON
San Clemente, California, July 2007

ACKNOWLEDGMENTS

Corwin Press would like to thank the following peer reviewers for their editorial insight and guidance:

Stephen Valentine
English teacher, 9–12
Montclair Kimberley Academy
Montclair, NJ

April Keck DeGennaro
Teacher Enrichment Specialist, K–8
Fayette County Georgia Board of Education
Fayetteville, GA

Amie Brown
Reading and Language Arts teacher, Seventh Grade
Coosa Middle School
Rome, GA

Katie Morrow
Elementary teacher, Fifth Grade
O'Neill Elementary School
O'Neill, NE

Virginia Montecino
Visiting Professor Emeritus of Education
George Mason University
Fairfax, VA

Beverly R. Plein
Technology Facilitator
National Milken Educator, NJ 2003
Benjamin Franklin Middle School
Teaneck, NJ

Dawn Butler
Goliad High School English III Teacher
Goliad High School
Goliad, TX

About the Author

Kristen J. Nelson is the author of numerous books in the educational field including *Teaching in the Digital Age* and *Developing Students' Multiple Intelligences.* She works for a large suburban school district in Orange County, California. Ms. Nelson was an elementary and middle school teacher before becoming an educational administrator. She lives with her husband and two daughters in San Clemente, California.

Introduction

Sometime in the late 1990s, the world changed. It was not a single moment in time; yet, it came quickly and almost unexpectedly. The world shifted from a culture centered on network television, phones with wires, and information on paper to a world centered on cable and satellite television, digital communications, and information on computer screens.

Although no anniversary marks this incredible transition, the United States became a digitized country competing in a digitized world—and there is no turning back. Worldwide, approximately 1.1 billion people use the Internet; in North America, 230 million use it. The Internet is no longer merely a novelty or simply an interesting way to spend time. It is used for shopping, consulting doctors, making investments, obtaining mortgages, tracking packages, checking out political candidates, researching, and communicating with others. Thirty years after it was created to help university and government workers connect, the Internet continues to grow. It still has a far distance to travel.

One area still under construction is the use of the Internet in education. The education world is at a crossroads—there is no better time to be living and working in a school. As educators integrate technology and the Internet into their classrooms, they also are becoming very aware of the current brain research and the theory of multiple intelligences that are opening doors for reaching and teaching students more effectively. These three tools—the Internet, brain research, and the theory of multiple intelligences—are transforming teaching and learning as nothing that has come before.

The purpose of *Teaching in the Digital Age: Using the Internet to Increase Student Engagement and Understanding, Second Edition* is to provide teachers with practical suggestions and ideas to use these tools to help students gain a deeper understanding of and knowledge about what they are learning. This book seeks to shed light on how these separate educational tools work together to help teachers make better use of their precious classroom time as they develop integrated lessons. There are many books on the theory of multiple intelligences, on brain research, and on the Internet; yet, few books explain how these three tools complement each other.

Rather than providing a collection of classroom lessons, *Teaching in the Digital Age: Using the Internet to Increase Student Engagement and Understanding, Second Edition* presents a mosaic of educational theory and practice to help teachers design their own classroom lessons that are powerful, based on brain research, and promote student understanding. This book uses the Understanding by Design framework proposed by Grant Wiggins and Jay McTighe[1] (1998/2005) to provide a scaffolding that teachers can use when designing Internet activities using the multiple intelligences theory and brain research. The Understanding by Design framework serves as an umbrella, constantly bringing lesson design back to the core concept of what teachers really want students to learn and understand. With this big picture in mind, the Internet, brain-compatible classroom concepts, and the theory of multiple intelligences become powerful supporting players in this challenging game of education.

THE SCOPE OF THIS BOOK

This book provides a deep and complex examination of the use of the Internet in the classroom by creating a larger framework in which the Internet, brain research, and the theory of multiple intelligences can play their roles in the overall educational process. It places the Internet in perspective—no longer as the new kid on the block, but as a substantial partner in the educational process. The Internet is not an island unto itself; teachers now recognize how it can work side-by-side with activities designed to awaken and strengthen students' intelligences. By doing this, students can be engaged and motivated like never before. Yet this book also focuses on the fact that engagement is only half of the puzzle; effectiveness is the other half. Internet-based activities that engage learners through a variety of intellectual stimulation must also be designed within the larger framework of what teachers want students to learn and be able to do.

There are literally hundreds of ways the Internet can be used with students to increase learning and understanding. To help organize the myriad projects and activities, this book uses three main categories developed by Judi Harris[2] (1998), who has been on the forefront of providing insight into how teachers can use the Internet in the classroom. The three main categories include interpersonal exchange, information-gathering and analysis, and problem-solving Internet activities. Although specific lesson plans are used as illustrations, the book seeks to provide activity scaffolding so that teachers may be empowered to design their own Internet-based instructional activities. Teachers will be able to create lessons based on what their students need to know and to adapt lessons to students' differing intelligences and learning needs. The theory of multiple intelligences and the principles of brain compatibility are woven throughout the book and are integrated directly into discussions about Internet projects.

Chapter 1 provides a lesson design process to help teachers integrate the theory of multiple intelligences, brain-compatible learning research, the Understanding by Design framework, and the Internet to create powerful lessons. A brief discussion on how to evaluate Web sites is also included in this chapter. Finally, an example lesson helps teachers get students started on learning about their different intelligences.

Chapter 2 introduces brain research principles that apply to the learner, examines the multiple intelligences theory of Gardner (1983), reviews the Internet briefly, and provides readers with an explanation of the Understanding by Design lesson design format developed by Grant Wiggins and Jay McTighe (1998/2005).

Chapter 3 looks at assessment and evaluation. This chapter focuses on how teachers can evaluate student understanding and develops several rubrics that can be used for any activity in this book. Rubrics for information literacy skills, Internet skills, and for multiple intelligences are provided to help teachers gain an understanding of how to best use rubrics in their instruction. The guiding principle of this chapter is the belief that assessment must be discussed with students before they work on an activity. This connects the assessment process to the instructional process.

Chapter 4 concentrates on providing information and practical suggestions to strengthen students' interpersonal exchange Internet skills. Information on skills such as using search engines, tips for making searches more effective, and guidance on using bookmarks is provided. E-mail, a powerful communication tool, is also discussed in relation to having students use it for instructional purposes. Interpersonal exchange activities are presented, offering interactive and challenging Internet activities for students to practice their Internet skills as they work in curricular areas.

Chapter 5 tackles a basic skill for the twenty-first century—information literacy. No book published on the Internet today should be without a discussion of this critical skill. With so much information at students' fingertips, students must learn to work effectively and productively with all types of information. Six information literacy skills are shared with classroom tips and a classroom lesson that provides students with practice for these skills. Suggestions for information-gathering and analysis Internet projects help teachers design Internet lessons that are based on their curriculum and that focus on giving students practice with their information literacy skills. These Internet projects also assist students in using and strengthening their multiple intelligences.

Chapter 6 begins with a focus on using questions to help direct classroom lessons and student activities. Different types of questions are featured as well as problem-solving Internet activities that employ questions to direct student learning. Again, these types of Internet activities are integrated with the multiple intelligences, enabling students to work in their different intelligences to solve problems and gain a deeper understanding of issues.

Appendix A includes a list of Web sites featured in this book as well as others of interest. Appendix B contains blank copies of rubrics used throughout the book. The bibliography includes references that support the material presented. Finally, an index concludes the book.

1

Designing Internet-Based Activities

In these days of high-stakes testing, laser focus on standards, and concerns about meeting the requirements of many state and federal laws, some teachers question whether they can afford the time to plan and teach an Internet-based lesson. This is understandable, as the pressures on teachers to cover so much material is huge. The important thing for teachers to know and remember is that students in classrooms nationwide are growing up in the digital age. They are naturally motivated through the use of technology. The more teachers integrate technology into their lessons, the more connected students' realities between school life and "real" life become.

Designing an effective Internet-based lesson comes easily when teachers realize it requires the same process of lesson planning they used long before the Internet came along. Teachers need to keep the big picture of what curriculum standards they want to reach and what they want students to learn and to have a good link to assessing whether these learning goals have been met. In this way, there is very little difference in lesson design, whether the Internet is used or not.

On the other hand, designing an Internet-based lesson requires teachers to bring a "wild card" to their lesson. Without the Internet, the teacher is in charge of collecting the material, disseminating information, controlling the discussion, and watching over the eventual end product. When the Internet comes into play, there are times when the teacher is asked to step aside and become an intellectual guide or facilitator. Students access information, collect their own material, have side discussions and connections, and watch over their eventual end product. In this sense, it is important for teachers to shift their thinking as they bring the Internet into their lesson-designing strategies. This chapter provides some practical suggestions for teachers as they work to bring Internet-based instruction into their classroom, baby step by baby step.

WHAT DOES A WELL-DESIGNED INTERNET ACTIVITY LOOK LIKE?

Before becoming enmeshed in the details of creating an activity, let us focus on the qualities of the activity that is being created. When a teacher creates a well-designed Internet activity, he or she strives to create an activity that demonstrates as many as possible of the following 15 components. Although by no means comprehensive, these 15 components are based on brain research and best practices and include ideas that lead to engaging and effective activities. While it is unlikely that an activity will include all of the components, the more an activity includes the better.

1. An activity is linked directly to curriculum standards. It is designed to have students work within the curriculum standards and makes students aware of what standards they are learning.
2. An activity is designed to foster deep understandings. It helps students gain deep understanding of a curriculum concept.
3. An activity is time efficient, yet allows students adequate completion time. It should not take months to complete, but students need to be given adequate time to work with it to gain understanding and go below the surface.
4. An activity is tied to students' prior knowledge. It allows students to access their prior knowledge about a subject to increase the meaning of what they are learning.
5. An activity is challenging, yet manageable. It challenges students' Internet, thinking, and problem-solving skills, yet it is not so difficult that they are unable to complete the project.
6. An activity has meaning and purpose. It has a specific purpose and is meaningful to students' lives. The content, the process, or the product must be meaningful for students.
7. An activity includes an emotional component. It has an emotional impact on students, yet it is not strong enough to cause students to shut down or be distracted. A link to personal interests assists in adding this emotional component.
8. An activity breeds curiosity in students. It must play off students' innate curiosity. The activity may begin with an open-ended question or may include interesting facts, baffle students, offer mystery, or puzzle them.
9. An activity provides choices or a sense of choice. It must give students the impression that they have some say or choice in the Internet activity. The activity may allow them several different assessment products to choose from or may provide a selection of Web sites to visit within the activity.
10. An activity uses the multiple intelligences. It provides students with opportunities to use and strengthen their multiple intelligences.

11. An activity is an opportunity for collaboration. It gives students opportunities to work with other students both in class and over the Internet on collaborative projects and activities.

12. An activity offers immediate feedback. It allows students to receive immediate feedback, guaranteeing that they are not practicing and ingraining misconceptions.

13. An activity provides time for reflection. It allows time for students to reflect on what they are learning with peers and other adults.

14. An activity offers a variety of assessments using standards and objectives. It includes an assessment directly linked to it, and standards and learning objectives are embedded into the assessment measure. This helps teachers if they are covering important standards and objectives. Assessment products are built around these standards, and students are to show their learning and growth relative to them. Activity worksheets and home-to-school correspondences can display standards prominently; teachers should discuss them frequently with students and parents.

15. An activity has a clear and final product. It should include an outcome or final product. Teachers should provide well-constructed models and products and give students clear due dates. The final target should always be within students' view.

UNDERSTANDING BY DESIGN FRAMEWORK

It is not enough to have a well-designed Internet activity. Each activity needs to be directly related to the curricular standards and be designed around how we know brains learn and retain information. To help teachers along this pathway of designing strong curriculum-based Internet activities, the Understanding by Design framework proposed by Wiggins and McTighe (1998/2005) can be used.

This framework provides a simple, yet powerful, means to organize Internet-based lessons. Students learn and understand the key concepts and skills from the lessons because teachers purposely and systematically link Internet activities to the concepts and skills they want students to learn and understand. As Wiggins and McTighe explain, "Students must perform effectively with knowledge to convince us that they really understand what quizzes and short-answer tests only suggest they get" (p. 82). Well-designed, thoughtful Internet activities can help students show us what they really know and deeply understand.

Frontward Versus Backward Lesson Design

Used by teachers for generations, traditional lesson design identifies a topic for study, uses activities to help students learn about the topic, and assesses students at the completion of the unit. This *frontward lesson design* format has stood the test of time. It promotes a sequence whereby the learning activities drive instruction. In other words, in this path to designing a lesson, when a teacher wants to teach a broad concept, the learning activities he or she develops usually drive the specifics of instruction. Figure 1.1 shows this frontward lesson design format.

Is there an alternative to allowing learning activities to drive instruction? The *backward lesson design* proposed in the Understanding by Design framework suggests the alternative is to have deep understandings and identified learning goals drive instruction. Instructional activities become a part of the process, a means to an end, rather than an end unto themselves. Figure 1.2 shows an example of backward lesson design with the Internet and multiple intelligences.

Major Components of the Understanding by Design Framework

The backward lesson design is based on three main components that work together seamlessly. Teachers first identify what students need to learn and understand; second, they determine and identify evidence of that learning; and third, they design learning activities to reach these goals and standards.

Identify What Students Need to Learn and Understand

Establishing curricular priorities—making choices about what to teach and when to teach it—is one of the most challenging tasks for teachers. These choices are especially challenging because teachers have much more to teach than they have time available to teach it in—especially with a long list of standards at each grade level. Both new and experienced teachers find that any unit of study involves numerous simultaneous learning targets: skills, knowledge, attitudes, abilities to manipulate and use information, and deep understandings to acquire.

Before teachers begin designing Internet-based instruction, it is critical for them to examine exactly what they want students to learn and, more important, why they are to learn it. The Understanding by Design framework distinguishes three levels of understanding to help teachers decide on what students need to learn.

Level 1: Information worth being familiar with. This information includes ideas that teachers want students to hear, read about, superficially examine, and briefly discuss. These items are easily assessed using traditional testing and assignment methods. For example, when students study about Egypt, they need to become familiar with the general location of the country and the important river that runs through it.

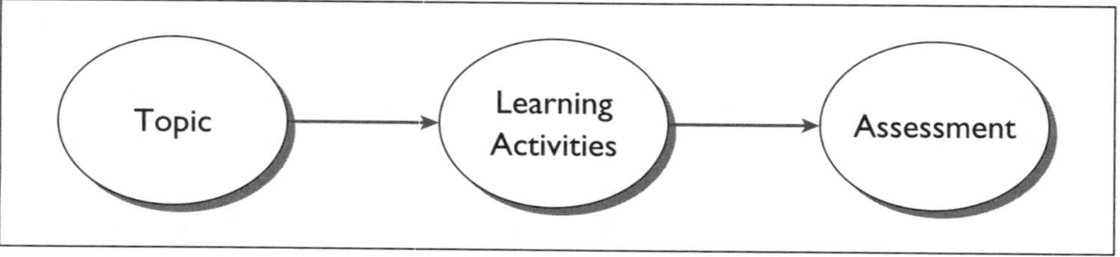

Figure 1.1

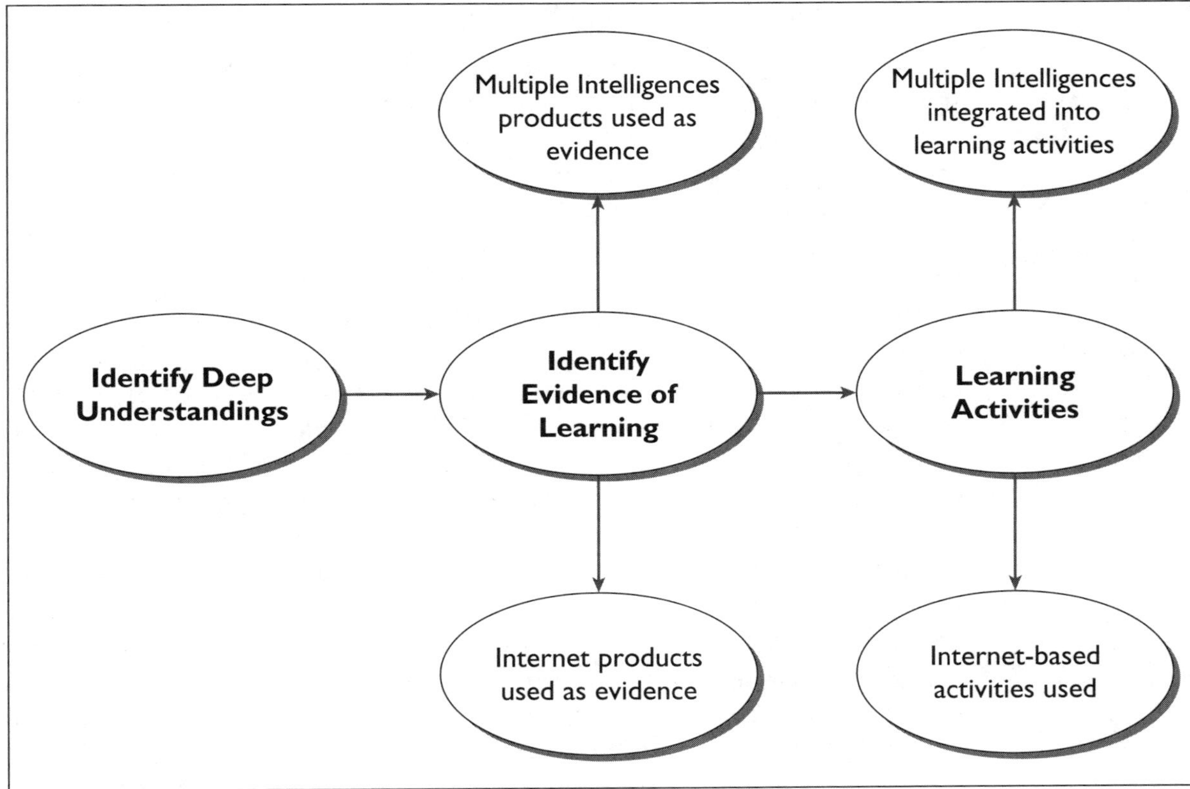

Figure 1.2

Level 2: Knowledge and skills important to know and do. These facts, concepts, and skills are identified by the teacher as necessary foundational knowledge so that students may accomplish a task at hand or complete a performance-based assignment. For example, when students study Egypt they may need to acquire knowledge about a specific period of history, understand the polytheistic beliefs of the Egyptians, and learn specific facts about the architecture so that they might continue on in the unit and participate in specific learning activities.

Level 3: Enduring understanding. This level of learning represents the big, important understandings that students will learn and continue to apply in their learning. These big concepts provide a framework for understanding the facts and surface knowledge that students may also learn. For example, a teacher may set a goal that students will understand the significant contributions ancient civilizations have made to the world and will be able to identify how those contributions have influenced their own lives.

Teachers must examine these three levels of learning and recognize what level a lesson is designed to teach. After self-monitoring for a few weeks, a teacher may find that most of his or her lessons target the first two levels without teaching or discussing any enduring understandings.

Determine and Identify Evidence of Learning

After teachers identify what students need to learn and understand in a lesson, the next step is to ask, What would count as evidence of this learning? Assessment choices can and need to be rich, demanding, and diverse. (*Note:* Following is a brief description of assessment; for a more thorough examination of assessment, see Chapter 3.)

Assessment measures help teachers evaluate if students understand and have reached the lesson's goals. Assessments include exams, authentic tasks and projects, quizzes and tests, informal checks for understanding, and student self-assessments. There is no one right way to assess; rather, it is important for teachers to remember that each child needs to create a photo album of assessment and evaluation. In other words, no one test or assessment measure provides a complete picture of a student's skills and knowledge. Instead, using a wide variety of assessments provides a balanced and accurate portrayal of a student's skills and knowledge base.

When looking at assessment measures, teachers need to keep several thoughts in mind. Through assessments directly linked to instruction, students need to show that they have increased their understanding about the concept. Assessments should go beyond simply providing black-or-white evaluations that search for right or wrong answers—they should also travel a gray timeline of assessing the many steps to understanding a concept. Can students explain the concept? Can they use their understanding to interpret and apply what they have learned? Can they show empathy toward others involved in the event they are studying? Assessment takes on an entirely new look when teachers begin to assess for understanding, not just for knowledge acquisition.

NINE STEPS TO A SUCCESSFUL INTERNET-BASED PROJECT

This section outlines for teachers how to design learning activities that are based on brain-compatible learning principles and that integrate multiple intelligences theory with Internet use in the classroom. There are nine suggested steps that implement the major components of the Understanding by Design framework to help teachers begin planning these types of activities. Teachers must remember to start slowly and start small. They should begin with easy-to-manage projects and move out from there. Teachers may start by using a unit that is taught each year and simply add one Internet component. By starting small, teachers not only learn to integrate the Internet into their curriculum, but also reduce the risk of being caught up in a great Internet project that has nothing to do with their curriculum or standards. Steps are matched with their appropriate section in the upcoming "Taking It to the Classroom" application examples by a notation in parentheses.

Step 1: Prepare for the Lesson (Brain Compatibility Link)

Teachers prepare by reviewing the brain-compatible learning principles (see Figure 2.2 in Chapter 2) as a reminder of the importance of designing lessons with these in mind. Teachers can identify the principles that most likely can be included in the project.

Step 2: Start With the End in Mind (Charting the Way)

Teachers decide the deep understandings and curriculum goals students need to learn. What content standard do students need to master and how can an Internet project facilitate this goal? Teachers may list the skills that need to be taught or reviewed and design projects around these skills. In addition, teachers decide how students' work will be assessed.

A particularly useful strategy for examining goals and outcomes is for teachers to answer six preplanning questions (see Figure 1.3). These questions integrate the Understanding by Design framework with Internet activities and the multiple intelligences theory. By using six questions as guides, teachers can create interesting, engaging, and powerful learning activities. Teachers who use these questions are assured that they are looking at the big picture of what students need to learn before they get involved in an exciting Internet activity. Preplanning questions help teachers guarantee that they are examining the important curriculum and assessment issues before getting swept away into Internet wonderland.

Step 3: Research Others' Internet Projects (Discovering Internet-Based Resources)

Teachers can go online to see how other teachers structure their Internet activities. Teachers may begin with the following Internet sites:

- Global SchoolNet Foundation (www.globalschoolnet.org/index.html)
- Education Place (primary) (www.eduplace.com)
- Classroom Connect (corporate.classroom.com)

(*Note:* Appendix A gives addresses of these and additional Web sites.)

Preplanning Questions for Activities

1. What are the deep understandings of this activity?
2. What skills and knowledge, both academic and Internet-based, will students strengthen as a result of this activity?
3. What facts do students need to become familiar with through this activity?
4. How can students' understanding, knowledge, and skills be assessed?
5. What type of Internet activity will help students reach these learning goals? What will the Internet activity entail? How long will the activity last?
6. What intelligences can be brought into this Internet activity to help students gain understanding?

Figure 1.3

Step 4: Choose the Type of Internet Project (Discovering Internet-Based Resources)

After teachers become familiar with online projects offered by other teachers, they revisit their curriculum standards understanding goals to develop the type, topic, and content for a project. Teachers also need to analyze what intelligences students will naturally use in the project and give students the opportunity to use additional intelligences by adding to or adjusting the project.

Designing a safe Internet project is an important part of planning for an activity. Many students are raised with a rattle in one hand and a mouse in the other. They show up in classrooms with a rich knowledge of the Internet and its power to entertain and provide information. Some teachers may feel intimidated by students' knowledge and ability to surf the Internet with the greatest of ease. Yet teachers must provide students with a large amount of guidance when it comes to the Internet. Before jumping in and using the Internet as a daily learning tool, teachers should consider a few important tips on developing safe Internet lessons:

- Students should be required to find very specific information, not just surf. Teachers should never start lessons by telling students to go surf the Internet.
- Students should always write down the URLs of the sites they use and report them in a bibliography format. (Information on how to cite Internet sources is discussed in Chapter 5.)
- Teachers need to avoid sending an entire class to the same site, as it may slow down the site allowing only some students to access the information.
- Teachers should have Web sites selected and previewed before students visit.
- Older students need to receive strict guidelines on sites that they cannot visit during their time at school. These sites would include chat rooms and social networking sites such as MySpace.com.

Evaluating Web sites is a survival skill for teachers who wish to use the Internet in the classroom. They must learn how to select and evaluate good Web sites based on curriculum goals. The selection process can literally make or break the activity and, consequently, greatly influence how much or how little students learn. In evaluating Web sites, teachers should ask 11 questions, discussed briefly here and shown in Figure 1.4.

1. Does the Web site help teachers meet the standards or understanding goals? Two primary goals are to help students reach or surpass the standards and gain a deeper understanding of the material. Teachers should remember these primary goals when deciding what Web resources to use.
2. Does the Web site allow for two-way interaction? Static displays are pretty, but Web sites should also include connections. Teachers should choose Web sites that allow the students to interact in some way. Interaction can include drawing, writing, clicking, or chatting. The Web site should offer something for students to do.

Web Site Evaluation Questions

1. Does the Web site help teachers meet the standards or understand goals?
2. Does the Web site allow for two-way interaction?
3. Is the Web site visually appealing?
4. Is the Web site easy to navigate?
5. Is the Web site fast loading?
6. Does the Web site allow students to publish their work or to display some final outcome?
7. Does the Web site activate more than one of the multiple intelligences?
8. Is the information on the Web site verifiable?
9. Is the Web site consistent with current brain-based teaching concepts?
10. Does the Web site meet the standard or understanding goal or could the standard or goal be met better using some other medium?
11. How recent is the information or research on the Web site?

Figure 1.4

Source: Adapted from Howard Gardner, *Multiple Intelligences:* New Horizons, 2006.

3. Is the Web site visually appealing? Media need not be dull and boring to be effective. Students enjoy themselves and are more willing to put forth additional effort if the activities and Web pages seem appealing.

4. Is the Web site easy to navigate? Sites must include good information, but they also need to be easy to navigate or students will waste too much time getting around a site. Teachers should choose sites with consistent navigation tools.

5. Is the Web site fast loading? Students might not wait for two minutes for a page to load before they will find other things to occupy their time. Some Web sites load more quickly than others due to their content and how they were created.

6. Does the Web site allow students to publish their work or display some final outcome? Computers make publishing simple. Students can publish their work on the Internet or print out materials they have typed up or drawn. Does the site lend itself to working with curriculum and understanding goals and not just surfing?

7. Does the Web site activate more than one of the multiple intelligences? Some sites are mainly textual and do not involve intelligences other than the verbal/linguistic intelligence. Better sites are interactive and include visuals, graphics, or music.

8. Is the information on the Web site verifiable? Is the information reliable and consistent? Is the material fact, or opinion without substantiation? Good Web sites include ways to verify facts within them. The information included in the site should be consistent with what is already known on the topic. If the site includes groundbreaking material, it should be well documented. Sites based on opinions are not necessarily bad. However, they may confuse students as they can seem to present factual information that is not substantiated or is simply someone's opinion.
9. Is the Web site consistent with current brain-based teaching concepts? Does the site stir students' emotions? Is the site interesting to students? Does the site chunk information for better retention? Does the site build on students' prior knowledge? Is the information presented meaningful to students?
10. Does the Web site meet the standard or understanding goal or could the standard or goal be better met using some other medium? Web resources are only one of many ways to reach curriculum objectives. Many students are very motivated by using the Internet, but teachers should use a Web site only if it is the best way to cover the learning objectives.
11. How recent is the information or research on the Web site? Students need to learn how to analyze the age of a Web site and its information. This can be done by finding a date(s) on the Web site itself or by cross-referencing the information with other sites.

Appendix B presents these 11 criteria in a Web Site Evaluation Form. Teachers can use the form to evaluate sites they wish to use with students.

Step 5: Start Small and Specific (Stepping Out)

Teachers can design the project with specific understandings, goals, skills, and outcomes. The more specific and the more closely aligned with traditional instructional goals, the better. Teachers need to remember to start small—allow practice and time to improve the Internet skills used in the instruction process. Teachers should create starter projects that are small and specific and when these are completed, should then consider creating larger, more complex Internet projects.

Step 6: Set Due Dates (Stepping Out)

Teachers need to identify specific beginning and ending dates for the project and set deadlines for students' responses. Teachers should create a timeline of important deadlines and dates. If a teacher decides to post a project on the Internet so that others may participate, he or she must give enough lead time between the announcement of the project and its launch date.

Step 7: Give Feedback to Students (Stepping Out)

Teachers can provide ongoing checkpoints and discussion time between themselves and individual students to monitor students' progress on the projects, to chart students' progress toward meeting the curriculum standards and understanding goals, and to determine how well students are using their different intelligences. If teachers give immediate feedback and use ongoing assessment, students can adjust and change as necessary to reach their learning goals. Teachers can remind themselves that immediate feedback is a strong brain-compatible learning component.

Step 8: Share the Results (Stepping Out)

Teachers can provide opportunities for students to share their Internet projects and activities with other students in the class. This provides students with valuable experience using their speaking skills as well as honing their technological presentation skills. Students can also be asked to explain what intelligences they used in the project and give examples of when and how they were used and strengthened. Students may also be asked to share their final projects with their parents by posting them on the Internet or sending them via e-mail.

Step 9: Reflect On and Celebrate Learning (Stepping Out)

After all projects have been shared and the curriculum understanding and learning goals have been met, teachers can allow time for students to reflect on and celebrate their learning. Providing time for reflection allows students to store their learning in their long-term memories and see their learning within a larger context. Teachers can celebrate by acknowledging and reflecting on specific students' work and by pointing out how much students' understandings and skills have progressed.

EXAMPLE LESSON: GETTING STARTED

To highlight the lesson design process using the nine steps and to provide a practical example of how designing lessons in this way can work, a beginning lesson for upper elementary and secondary students is given next. This lesson teaches students about their multiple intelligences using the Internet as an information delivery system.

This example lesson uses the same format that is used for all classroom applications—called Taking It to the Classroom—throughout the book. After a brief introduction to the activity, the lesson begins with Brain-Compatibility Link, identifying brain-compatibility foci. The lesson continues with Charting the Way, including preplanning questions teachers use to identify the deep understandings and knowledge they want students to learn and to consider appropriate assessment methods. (Assessment measures are discussed in more detail in Chapter 3.) Next is Discovering Internet-Based Resources, identifying appropriate Web sites. The lesson ends with Stepping Out, detailing actual lesson activities.

Taking It to the Classroom

So Many Ways to Be Smart!

The following lesson provides students in Grades 5 through 10 with an introduction to the multiple intelligences. Teaching students about the different intelligences can be a starting point for any classroom. This lesson provides students with information about the intelligences and experiences within each intelligence. Students use the Internet to access information about the theory of multiple intelligences.

Brain-Compatibility Link

Focus Links: Safe and Nurturing Environment; Reflection

This lesson teaches students how their brains work and validates their individual cognitive strengths. This lesson contributes to a *safe and nurturing* environment for students—the type of environment that brain research studies show to be important to learning. A safe and nurturing environment allows students to feel unafraid to take risks and helps students accept and appreciate individual differences. After all, one of the most threatening environments is one where everyone is supposed to think and act alike and the person who does not is singled out and possibly ridiculed. Therefore, at the heart of this brain-compatible learning environment is the acceptance that everyone has his or her own strengths and weaknesses and that difference is truly good. This lesson is a starting point in helping students create a safe, nurturing, and caring environment.

In addition, this lesson encourages teachers to schedule time at the completion of the lesson for students to *reflect* on their learning and share their work with the class. This reflection time is critical for helping students process information and store it in their memories for future use.

Charting the Way

Q1. What are the deep understandings of this activity?

Students understand that there are multiple ways of being smart and that their own brain includes these multiple intelligences.

Q2. What skills and knowledge, both academic and Internet-based, will students strengthen as a result of this activity?

Students strengthen their academic research skills as they locate information on the Internet related to the different intelligences and analyze the information for usefulness and practicality. Students also practice their Internet searching skills as they learn what a URL address is, how to type it in, and how to use it to locate information.

Q3. What facts do students need to become familiar with through this activity?

Students become familiar with the eight multiple intelligences.

Q4. How can students' understanding, knowledge, and skills be assessed?

The So Many Ways to Be Smart! Rubric (Figure 1.5) provides an assessment method to help guide students in their activity. Students need to know they will be assessed for their understanding and knowledge of the different intelligences by how well their end product (mind map, report, or role play) displays the depth and complexity of their understanding. It does not matter how pretty the mind map is or how funny the role play is. What matters is that the mind map, report, or role play shows the teacher that the student understands the different intelligences.

Teachers must remember that students need frequent and consistent exposure to and experiences in the different intelligences to gain a deep understanding of them. This introductory activity allows students to gain an awareness of the intelligences at the same time they learn how to use the Internet and the different intelligences in their final product.

To use this rubric, teachers can first share it with students. After students understand how they will be assessed using this rubric, they are responsible for showing the teacher that they have covered the assessment components in their work.

Q5. What type of Internet activity will help students reach these learning goals? What will the Internet activity entail? How long will the activity last?

Students, in pairs, use an information searching process and are provided with URL addresses for Internet sites that have explanations and examples of the different intelligences. Students find information that helps them learn about the different intelligences and complete their assessment activities. Teachers may consider using a worksheet to provide Web site locations and directions to students.

Q6. What intelligences can be brought into this Internet activity to help students gain understanding?

- *Verbal and Linguistic:* Students work with text to gain information about the intelligences.
- *Visual and Spatial:* Students create mind maps to show their understanding.
- *Interpersonal:* Students pair up to discuss how the intelligences play a role in human interactions and relationships.

The assessment outcomes are designed purposely to provide students with different avenues to show their learning using a variety of intelligences.

So Many Ways to Be Smart! Rubric			
	Masterful	**Skilled**	**Basic**
Application of knowledge in report, role play, or mind map	• Is able to apply knowledge and understanding with fluency and flexibility. • Is able to use knowledge in end product. • The end product completed with neatness, clarity, and showing understanding of content.	• Is able to perform well with knowledge in a limited way. • The end product is done well, yet lacks complexity of thinking. • The end product is neat and easy to follow.	• Only able to apply knowledge with help from the teacher or others or by relying on clearly laid out skills and procedures. • The end product is completed, yet lacks neatness, clarity, or complexity.
Explanation of Intelligences	• A thorough and inventive explanation is fully supported.	• Explanation that reflects some in-depth ideas but needs more evidence.	• Superficial explanation is more descriptive than analytical.
Internet Skills	• Is able to follow directions independently and participate in Internet activity with little or no guidance • Understands the Internet's role in activity. • Is able to focus on the Internet as a tool within the learning activity—not as an end to itself.	• Is able to follow directions with minor guidance and assistance. • Uses the Internet to learn curriculum topic. • Continues to refine Internet skills to make this learning smoother.	• Requires constant help in using the Internet. • Is unable to participate in the activity without breaking the flow to ask for help. • Focuses on the Internet procedures more than the curricular activity.
Use of Multiple Intelligences	• Uses a variety of intelligences in a complex and thoughtful way and articulates what intelligences are being used and why each was necessary for success of the project.	• Uses a variety of intelligences, yet is unaware of the roles each plays in the project's success. • Needs guidance in the use of one or two intelligences.	• Uses one or two intelligences in a basic or simplistic fashion, but is unaware of the uses of different intelligences. • Needs repeated guidance and assistance in all intelligences.

Figure 1.5

Discovering Internet-Based Resources

The Web sites are used by both students and teachers to research the theory of multiple intelligences. Teachers visit the sites to preview the information and find additional links and sites on multiple intelligences. These sites were selected because of their ease in explaining this theory, as well as providing clear definitions and examples of each intelligence. Several sites include excellent links that can expand both teacher and student research.

- I Think . . . Therefore . . . MI (www.surfaquarium.com/mi)
- Intelligence in Seven Steps (www.newhorizons.org/future/Creating_the_Future/crfut_gardner.html)
- Describing Intelligences in Students (www.ascd.org/ed_topics/2000armstrong/chapter3.html)
- Multiple Intelligences (www.thomasarmstrong.com/multiple_intelligences.htm)

Stepping Out

Teachers use the following steps to guide the lesson process:

1. Introduce the multiple intelligences theory to students using Figure 1.6. Take time to discuss each intelligence.
2. Explain that the theory was first proposed by Howard Gardner of Harvard University in 1983. Gardner believes there are eight intelligences and that people use them at different levels.
3. Pair students. Explain to students that they are going to learn more about the theory of multiple intelligences by visiting several Web sites that provide information and examples.
4. Share and review the selected assessment methods and rubric with students. Tell students that, after they have learned about this theory in greater detail through this activity, they will select one way to show that they have learned about this theory and the different intelligences. Allow them to choose between the following three assessment measures:
   a. Write a report defining each intelligence that includes examples of skills involved in that intelligence and describes famous individuals who are strong in the intelligence.

(Continued)

(Continued)

b. Role-play interviews of famous individuals who demonstrate strength in different intelligence areas. In role play, students choose a famous historical character to study and then "become" that character in a short skit with a few other students. Students need to concentrate on what intelligences the chosen character used in his or her life. Each group should have a balance of historical figures that represent a variety of intelligences. Students can also be asked to write a two-page mock interview with this person to show what they learned about this individual's multiple intelligences.

c. Create a detailed and extensive idea web or mind map with descriptions of each intelligence with supporting information for each. A mind map begins with a circle in the middle of the page with the label "Multiple Intelligences." Then, eight lines radiate from the circle, each labeled for an intelligence. Students add pieces of information about each intelligence at the end of its line. For example, the line labeled "Logical/Mathematical" could have several drawings and descriptive words, such as "good with numbers" and "able to see patterns" attached to it.

5. Allow students time to research the theory of multiple intelligences on the Internet and point them in the direction of the previewed Web sites.

6. After students have completed their chosen assessments, ask them to reflect on their learning by sharing their end product with the class.

Do You Know How Smart You Are?

The multiple intelligences theory was first proposed by Dr. Howard Gardner of Harvard University in 1983. This theory proposes that humans have more than one intelligence. Dr. Gardner believes that there are eight intelligences and that people use them at different levels. The eight intelligences include:

- **Verbal/Linguistic:** The ability to read, write, tell stories, memorize, think in words, and orally communicate
- **Logical/Mathematical:** The ability to work with numbers, do mathematics, compute, reason, apply logic, solve problems, and work with patterns
- **Visual/Spatial:** The ability to read and use maps, charts, drawings, mazes, and puzzles; imagine things, visualize; build; and design
- **Musical/Rhythmic:** The ability to sing, pick up sounds, remember melodies and rhythms, play an instrument, and listen to music
- **Bodily/Kinesthetic:** The ability to perform in athletics, dance, act, work in crafts, use tools, and develop hand-eye coordination
- **Interpersonal:** The ability to understand people, lead, organize, communicate, and resolve conflicts
- **Intrapersonal:** The ability to understand one's self, recognize one's strengths and weaknesses, set goals, and reflect
- **Naturalist:** The ability to understand nature, make distinctions, and identify flora and fauna

Figure 1.6

Using the Understanding by Design framework with the power of the multiple intelligences theory and the Internet places unlimited resources in the hands of teachers. The Understanding by Design framework provides a scaffolding for lessons that include the Internet, brain-compatible learning principles, and the multiple intelligences theory.

2

Connecting Brain-Compatible Learning, Multiple Intelligences, and the Internet

To help teachers design creative and personalized Internet-based lessons, this chapter focuses on concepts that range from brain compatibility research and the multiple intelligences theory to an overview about the Internet. Its purpose is to introduce these concepts as the bases for developing classroom applications.

BRAIN-COMPATIBLE LEARNING

The 1990s were called the "Decade of the Brain" by many. This is indeed difficult to dispute. Advances in technology in the neurosciences vastly improved how the human brain may be studied. These advances centered on brain imaging techniques that allow neuroscientists to actually watch the brain at work. For example, the PET scan uses radioactive glucose to gauge blood flow through the brain as various areas are activated. This provides researchers with information about where and how an experience or problem is processed in the brain. MRI looks at chemical differences in the composition of different tissues of the brain. Another familiar and well-used brain-imaging technique, the EEG, uses electrical transmissions to study brain patterns.

One of the greatest challenges in education is to use research gathered through these technologies in practical ways in the classroom to help children learn. This is no easy feat. It is much easier to stay the same course and continue doing things the way they have always been done. Yet, educational pioneers push teachers onward and upward in using new information about the brain. The term *brain compatible* was first used by Leslie Hart (1983) in his book, *Human Brain, Human Learning*. He challenged the education community to make teaching and learning more compatible with how the brain learns and processes information. Susan Kovalik and Karen Olsen (2002) expanded on these concepts in their book, *Exceeding Expectations: A User's Guide to Implementing Brain Research in the Classroom*. Writers adding to the wealth of knowledge and ideas on brain-compatible learning include Marzano (2003), Fogarty (2001), Wolfe (2001), Sylwester (1995), and Sousa (2006), to name just a few.

Numerous books and articles are available to educators that relate directly to brain-compatible learning. Yet, educators are still searching for how to relate these ideas to specific curriculum domains. The concepts and ideas of brain-compatible learning are still in their infancy. For the sake of this book, an amalgamation of many individuals' work is used to define the major tenets of brain-compatible learning. These are the most important ones for lesson design:

- *Meaning and Relevance:* One of the brain's important jobs is to seek meaning and relevance in everything it does. If a student does not see meaning or relevance in a lesson, his or her brain automatically begins looking for something that has more meaning (possibly slipping a note to a fellow student or sending a spitball across the room to an enemy). Students find meaning and relevance one way or another. Although this seems like a simple concept, it is really one of the most important ones and serves as a foundation for all other brain-compatible learning ideas. Teachers themselves can think of many workshops where they have been bored or maybe even escaped out the back door because what was being taught was perceived to be not relevant or meaningful to them. Seeking meaning and relevance is what drives human learning.

- *Emotions:* Emotions play a central role in learning and memory and therefore are a gateway to learning. The emotional part of the brain is located in the amygdala, which stores emotional information and acts as a file cabinet for all the experiences people have in life. When new information comes in, it travels through the amygdala and, if it has emotional content, is processed, filed, and sorted into memory. Emotional memory is one of the strongest memory systems humans possess.

- *Repetition and Rehearsal:* Learning and memory are reinforced through hearing, seeing, and experiencing the information repeatedly. In order for a student to make sense and meaning of new learning, he or she needs adequate time to process and reprocess it. This continuing reprocessing is critical to the transference of the information from short-term to long-term memory.

• *Prior Knowledge:* New learning builds on past learning and prior knowledge. When students learn new information, they instantly process the information for relevance and relationship to other pieces of information they have already learned. If there is indeed prior knowledge about the subject, the brain is able to more readily store the information in its memory. If there is no prior knowledge, the information can lack meaning and relevance to the learner. Therefore, it is important for teachers to help students link new information to their prior knowledge.

• *Adequate Time:* The brain needs time to process information. It is important for teachers to build time into each lesson for students to process and work with the information and skills they are learning. This can be done by giving students more time to work in an activity, stretching out a lesson's overall time schedule, or allowing for wait time before calling on students for an answer. By providing this time, students are able to rehearse and repeat what they have learned, make connections to prior knowledge, and reflect on their learning. Without adequate time, the new information is unlikely to ever make it into long-term memory storage because of the lack of connection and meaning.

• *Immediate Feedback:* The brain learns best when given feedback during the learning process. This feedback is most powerful when it is given during or immediately after the lesson. The brain is able to use this feedback to make the necessary changes instead of having time to repeatedly practice something incorrectly. Without immediate feedback, the new learning is seen as not relevant and important, hindering new connections and memory storage.

• *Collaboration:* The brain is social by nature and enjoys learning and reflecting on learning with others. Human beings are social creatures, and teachers need to recognize that learning does not take place in a vacuum but in social settings in which the brain has time to process information with others. This is especially true for individuals who are strong in the interpersonal intelligence and rely on their social interactions to process new information.

• *Reflection:* The brain needs time to reflect on what has been learned so that it may store the new information in its memory system for later retrieval. If the brain is unable to reflect on learning, it is difficult if not impossible for it to store the information in its long-term memory system. Many adults acknowledge the fact that what they remember long term is information and knowledge that they spent a lot of time working with and reflecting on. By reflecting on learning, the brain is able to scrutinize, observe, sort, synthesize, and connect new information to prior knowledge. During this reflection process, the brain is able to reorganize itself based on new information being learned.

• *Safe and Nurturing Environment:* The brain thrives on a climate of safety, caring, and low stress. This occurs mainly because, when humans are in an environment that is not safe and might contain a high level of stress, their limbic systems are activated. This system, one of the oldest in brain development, uses the emotional part of the brain to activate "flight or fight" responses. If humans feel threatened, the release of stress hormones such as cortisol may cause interruptions in the processing of information and therefore of the learning process. By being in a safe and nurturing environment, these stress hormones are not released, enabling the brain to concentrate on learning and remembering.

- *Active Learning:* Concepts and information learned must be actively used so that the brain transfers learning from short-term to long-term memory. If students simply sit and listen to information and have no active participation with it, they may quickly forget the information because it lacks meaning and relevancy. This is why many—even teachers—struggle to remember five things they learned in their American History high school class. In contrast, active learning helps students make meaning of new information. It increases motivation to learn and helps students develop connections with other knowledge and information.

- *Choice:* The brain thrives on choice. Motivation is increased when the learner chooses what to learn instead of learning what others say is important. This empowerment increases meaning and relevancy to the learner, therefore increasing the level of motivation to learn and remember the new information.

- *Pattern Seeking:* The brain is a pattern-seeking machine. It constantly seeks patterns in information and learning experiences and is able to use these patterns to file the new information in its memory system. The brain uses these patterns to make connections that help make sense of new learning, enabling the brain to organize the information in a way that is meaningful.

- *Chunking:* The chunking of information helps the learner organize and retain the information because a set of data is perceived as a single item, just as the reader currently sees *chunking* as one word instead of eight letters. By chunking information, less working memory is used, allowing for more information to be processed at a time. As working memory's capacity is enhanced, the learner is better able to associate chunks of information in a meaningful way.

MULTIPLE INTELLIGENCES THEORY

In addition to information from the brain research community, teachers can improve their understanding of how students learn by examining the theory of multiple intelligences, which was proposed by Dr. Howard Gardner (1983) of Harvard University in *Frames of Mind: The Theory of Multiple Intelligences*. Gardner derived his theory from extensive brain research, including interviews, tests, and studies of hundreds of individuals. He studied the cognitive profiles of stroke and accident victims, prodigies, autistic individuals, those with learning disabilities, idiot savants, and people from diverse cultures. He concluded that intelligence is not one fixed trait that dominates all the skills and problem-solving abilities a person possesses. Gardner's theory does not question the existence of a general intelligence but does probe the possibilities of intelligences not covered by a single concept of intelligence. His research suggests that intelligence is centered in many different areas of the brain, which are interconnected, rely on one another, work independently when needed, and can be developed with the right environmental conditions.

Gardner defines an intelligence as comprising three main components: (1) the ability to create an effective product or offer a service that is valuable in one's culture; (2) a set of skills that enables an individual to solve problems encountered in life; and (3) the potential for finding or creating solutions for problems, enabling a person to acquire new knowledge. The intelligences Gardner recognizes include verbal and linguistic, logical and mathematical, visual and spatial, bodily and kinesthetic, musical and rhythmic, interpersonal, intrapersonal, and naturalist. Each intelligence area is demonstrated through specific talents, skills, and interests (see Figure 2.1). The fact that these intelligences can be nurtured and strengthened has a monumental influence on how students can be taught for maximum learning and achievement.

As brain research continues to provide information that educators never dreamed of knowing, the multiple intelligences theory adds to this wealth of information. Although the multiple intelligences theory has powerful implications for the world of education, it is not an educational prescription. There is no one way to use it in the classroom, and there is no one way to use it with the Internet. It is important to remember that many of the strongest neural networks are formed by the experience of involving students in solving authentic problems in their school (Wolfe, 2001).

Through the lens of multiple intelligences, teachers see students as more capable as they demonstrate learning in a multitude of ways. Students are given the opportunity to be acknowledged for their strengths—for what they can do well. This new approach can literally change the way teachers view students—turning an average student into a genius as his or her teacher legitimately acknowledges the amazing ways this child processes information and produces knowledge. This overall teaching philosophy adds to the richness and complexity of a classroom as a wider variety of experiences and ways of thinking and processing information are honored.

At Russell Elementary School in Lexington, Kentucky, the staff chose to move the entire school into an education program based on multiple intelligences. One of the powerful structures they have put in place is the Cycle of Success (Campbell & Campbell, 1999). This cycle encourages teachers to teach to students' strengths and to personalize education. The cycle of success begins when teachers are trained to observe students' multiple intelligences and learn to perceive each student's strengths. Teachers then personalize instruction for their students, a step that leads to success. The cycle provides a simple yet powerful way to guarantee students' academic and social success.

The multiple intelligences theory provides a foundation to personalize instruction and recognize student strengths. In discussing the ways his theory relates to education, Gardner recognizes that the multiple intelligences theory can be used in the classroom in the following three ways:

1. to cultivate desired capabilities and talents in students;
2. to approach a concept, subject matter, or discipline in a variety of ways; and
3. to personalize education as human differences are taken seriously.

Multiple Intelligences		
Intelligence	**Talents, Skills, and Interests**	**Learning Activities**
Verbal/Linguistic	reading, writing, telling stories, memorizing, thinking in words, oral communication	reading, hearing, and seeing words; speaking; writing; discussing; debating
Logical/Mathematical	working with numbers, doing math, computing, reasoning, logic, problem solving, finding patterns	working with patterns and numbers, classifying, categorizing, working with the abstract
Visual/Spatial	using maps and charts, drawing, completing mazes and puzzles, imagining things, visualizing, building, designing	working with pictures and colors, using mind's eye, drawing and creating visual representations
Bodily/Kinesthetic	participating in athletics, dancing, acting, doing crafts, using tools, possessing hand-eye coordination	touching, moving, processing knowledge through bodily sensations
Musical/Rhythmic	singing, picking up sounds, remembering melodies, playing rhythms, playing an instrument, listening to music	singing, listening to music and melodies, playing rhythm, putting information to song
Interpersonal	understanding people, leading, organizing, communicating, resolving conflicts, joining groups	cooperative learning, sharing, comparing, relating, interviewing, working with peers
Intrapersonal	understanding self, recognizing strengths and weaknesses, setting goals, reflecting	working alone, completing self-paced and independent activities, having own space, reflecting
Naturalist	understanding nature, making distinctions, identifying flora and fauna	working in nature, exploring living things, learning about plants and natural events

Figure 2.1

All three of these uses can be fostered and strengthened by integrating the multiple intelligences theory in brain-compatible classrooms with the powerful instructional tool of the Internet. Many ask if the theory of multiple intelligences really helps students learn better. It is a simple question without a simple answer, yet research shows great promise. Linda and Bruce Campbell (1999), in their book *Multiple Intelligences and Student Achievement: Success Stories From Six Schools*, reported that when schools and classrooms implement instructional programs based on the theory of multiple intelligences, achievement scores do indeed show great growth. The six schools the Campbells studied, ranging from elementary to high schools, went beyond anecdotal stories to show growth on actual standardized tests and classroom-based assessments.

THE INTERNET

As teachers continue to learn more about how the brain works, they are also being challenged to learn about and use the Internet in their instructional practice. The Internet has revolutionized communications like nothing before it. The invention of the telegraph, telephone, radio, and computer set the stage for an integration of powerful communication tools. The Internet is at once a worldwide broadcasting center, a mechanism for disseminating information, and a medium for collaborating between individuals and their computers without regard for geographic location.

The Internet represents a myriad of tools for students. It can function as a library, an encyclopedia, or simply as a replacement for pencil and paper. It can serve as a telephone, deliver mail like a mailman, and act as a file cabinet for collections of information. Most of all, it can be overwhelming and, at times, frustrating if students are not taught how to navigate this expansive source of information. As students become adept at navigating the Internet, they need to know what to do with all of the information, knowledge, and personal links that the Internet delivers to their fingertips.

The Internet has slowly trickled into classrooms throughout the United States, and what once seemed unique and rare is now ubiquitous for most teachers and students. Seen as threatening by many educators at one time, the Internet has become a useful and important teacher's aide in many classrooms. The Internet is one of the most powerful and rewarding instructional tools available for teachers. Within seconds, an entire civilization or country thousands of miles away is delivered to a teacher's desktop. Questions that would have taken hours to answer are not only answered but also expounded upon. Because of its timeliness and currency, the Internet can capture teachable moments. As students' eyes light up with excitement, the Internet can expand a teachable moment with pictures, facts, and human stories that make learning come alive.

The Internet provides a wealth of resources and information that make teaching exciting and new. Just a few of the things that can be found on the Internet include:

- lesson plans
- virtual field trips
- blogs
- telementors
- Podcasts
- book reviews
- historical archives
- information about authors, artists, and others
- science fair projects
- songs and stories
- tutorials
- simulations
- music
- facts, figures, and formulas
- exhibits
- experiments
- maps
- collaborative projects

- seminars for professional development
- electronic publishing
- collaborative problem-solving activities
- electronic appearances

Yet even with all of these Internet additions, educators have quickly realized that the Internet does not necessarily improve education in the classroom. The Internet is merely a tool, just as a pencil is a tool. A pencil can be used to write the great American novel, tap a beat on a table, or poke someone in the eye. The Internet is similar. It can be used as a powerful educational tool, but only if it capitalizes on new understandings of how the human brain learns.

Does the Internet increase student learning? This question has haunted the educational community since the Internet made its way into classrooms. In his article "Technology and Achievement: The Bottom Line," Harold Wenglinsky (2006) states,

> Results from the NAEP assessments in mathematics, science, and reading for 4th and 8th graders indicated that the quality of computer work was more important than the quantity. Students could receive a substantial benefit, no benefit, or even negative consequences from working with computers in the classroom, depending on how their teachers chose to use technology. Using computers to help students work through complex problems, thus tapping higher-order thinking skills, produced greater benefits than using computers to drill students on a set of routine tasks. (p. 30)

Educators can conclude that how students use computers is more important than how often they have access to this technology. Technology should be seen as simply one in an array of classroom tools rather than as the focus of the classroom. Teachers can take this instructional tool and use it with what they know about brain research and the theory of multiple intelligences to make the learning process more powerful, meaningful, and memorable.

In the past decade, standards and accountability have increased dramatically, dominating the discussion in education at all levels. This laser focus has made the link between curriculum, standards, and technology more important to find. In his article, "Digital Content and the Curriculum," Hoff (1999) states, "The need for better links between digital content and curricula is driven by the convergence of two major trends in education—state officials are increasingly prescribing what should be taught in the classroom, through academic standards and high-stakes tests; at the same time, they're encouraging greater use of technology" (p. 51).

At first glance, these two trends might seem adversarial. In this day and age of standards and high-stakes testing, many teachers feel they do not have the time to figure out how to use technology in the curriculum. Yet teachers who do figure out how to use technology for these tasks soon find there is no going back. When technology becomes integrated into the daily curriculum, the power of this tool can really help students learn and remember important information and skills.

The bottom line is that a direct link must be formed between what students need to learn and how the Internet is used in instruction. Many Internet projects and activities are developed without this vital connection—with no direct link to standards and objectives and with no end learning goal. The failure to connect standards and the Internet is understandable. After all, teachers have found it difficult to say no to an Internet activity that, for example, puts a class in communication with a biologist at the South Pole studying penguins even when few, if any, standards or learning objectives relate specifically to penguins.

Some classrooms engage in work that is hands-on without being minds-on. When using the Internet, teachers may find it especially easy to simply require students to experience, rather than *learn* and *understand.* Teachers may feel caught in a catch-22 situation—they race the calendar to cover material, feeling pressured to teach by mentioning it or by surfing it via the Internet.

Brain-Compatible Learning and the Internet

Figure 2.2 includes the most applicable brain-compatible learning components and how they relate to using the Internet in the classroom. Teachers can improve students' learning if they are aware of this direct link between these concepts and the Internet. The Internet in and of itself is not necessarily brain compatible, but how a teacher uses the Internet in the instruction process can most definitely be compatible with how students' brains work.

As teachers become aware of how brain-compatible learning components can work seamlessly with the Internet, they can design activities and experiences that provide students with powerful learning opportunities. No longer is the Internet a stand-alone educational tool; it may now take on greater importance as teachers are able to link it with how students' brains learn.

The Internet is also an ideal mechanism for encouraging students to assume responsibility for their own learning. As students find different learning resources on the Internet, they become active participants in their quest for knowledge. Incorporating the Internet into the classroom provides students with more opportunities to structure their own learning. Students can define their learning needs, find information, assess its value, build their own knowledge base, and communicate their discoveries. Finally, the Internet engages students in interactive learning. The Internet turns passive students into active participants—asking students on a regular basis to take information and turn it into knowledge.

Multiple Intelligences and the Internet

Separately, the Internet and the theory of multiple intelligences promise to help students learn more; when integrated, these two educational tools can promote student learning even more. When combined with strong, strategic teaching and the theory of multiple intelligences, the Internet can transform classrooms and create magical moments of learning.

One of the great promises of educational technology is that it will help teachers find individual pathways into students' brains. Recent advances in the quality of Internet projects and activities offer educators a real possibility for providing students with access to knowledge and information. A key to effectively using the Internet lies in recognizing and understanding that all students

Relating Brain-Compatible Learning Principles to Internet-Based Activities	
Brain-Compatible Principle	**Internet Relationship**
Meaning and Relevance: The brain seeks meaning and relevance in all it does.	Many Internet activities are problem based and ask students to research relevant and timely issues, collect data, or complete other tasks that relate to real-life issues.
Emotions: Positive emotions are critical to learning and memory; negative emotions hinder the learning process.	The Internet is fun, novel, and students feel in control. Students are stimulated by most Web sites that allow them to hear, see, and do content as they think for themselves.
Repetition and Rehearsal: Learning and memory are reinforced through consistent rehearsal and practice.	The Internet allows students to visit and revisit sites allowing for repetition and rehearsal of information.
Prior Knowledge: New learning is supported by prior knowledge.	Internet links allow learners to start and review basic concepts and build on those with additional links.
Adequate Time: The brain needs time to work with new learning and information.	Some Internet activities make time allowances for person-to-person communication as well as time to access Web sites. This virtual waiting time allows students to learn and reflect.
Immediate Feedback: The brain needs ongoing and consistent feedback during the learning process.	Internet activities can be shared electronically with mentors and classmates to provide immediate feedback. Person-to-person Internet activities also provide this type of feedback.
Collaboration: The brain is social by nature and enjoys learning and reflecting with others.	The Internet provides interpersonal communications and collaboration opportunities via e-mail, chat rooms, and bulletin boards.
Reflection: The brain needs reflection time to process and store new learning.	Internet activities can include a reflection component. Students can also reflect on their learning through e-mail and bulletin boards.
Safe and Nurturing Environment: For academic and social success, the brain needs a climate of safety, caring, and low stress.	With appropriate safety measures (e.g., firewalls, preselected Web sites, student search engines), the Internet provides a virtual environment that is safe and nurtures students' interests.
Active Learning: New learning must be used actively to transfer learning from short-term to long-term memory.	The Internet lends itself to active learning as students participate in collecting and working with information. Active manipulation of data and skills on a site requires students to do something with the information and aids in the transfer to long-term memory.
Choice: By giving students choices, their motivation and learning are increased.	The Internet provides a wide range of choices and selections throughout each site. In addition, Internet activities include giving students choices.
Pattern Seeking: The brain is a pattern-seeking machine and uses these patterns to file new information in its memory.	The Internet provides repetition of information found on different sites and the opportunity to link pieces of information together as different sites are explored.
Chunking: Chunking information helps the brain process new information.	Most Internet sites are designed with information naturally chunked into smaller sections.

Figure 2.2

Source: This list of characteristics compiles information from multiple sources including but not limited to Sylwester (1995), Sousa (2006), Caine and Caine (1991), and Kovalik and Olsen (2002).

have different intellectual profiles, and the use of the Internet needs to reflect that knowledge in well-constructed activities and projects.

The Internet provides learning opportunities for students to gain access to information using their multiple intelligences. For example, 10 years ago a student may have become disengaged and bored while listening to his or her teacher discuss the military strategies behind World War II. Today this same student can use the Internet to access the same information—he or she can watch an interactive video, study maps of Europe that show the different military positions, and read firsthand accounts of military action. This type of learning not only engages students but also motivates them to gain a deeper understanding of a concept or event.

Figure 2.3 shows the different types of Internet opportunities available to reinforce the multiple intelligences. It is important to remember that the intelligences do not work in isolation, but instead work together through a variety of tasks. Therefore, many intelligences and Internet activities overlap.

The Internet provides an avenue to strengthen each intelligence as students are asked to participate in activities and projects that foster cognitive and social growth. As teachers design learning experiences that reach out to their students' multiple intelligences through active engagement, student learning becomes more efficient and effective because it is consistent with natural brain operations. The Internet is an incredible tool for reaching all intelligences and reinforcing learning through these neural networks.

The Internet also allows students to take charge of their own learning through direct exploration, expression, and experience. This shifts the student's role from *being taught* to *learning* and the teacher's role from *expert* to *collaborator* or *guide*. As teachers make this important shift and use the theory of multiple intelligences with students, their classrooms increasingly become brain-compatible learning environments. With the growing amount of brain research available, teachers have a wonderful opportunity to integrate brain-compatible learning components and the Internet to provide powerful lessons to students.

By integrating the Internet with ongoing opportunities for engaging students' different intelligences, teachers provide students with learning activities that not only increase the personalization of instruction but also raise students' level of learning and retaining knowledge.

Short- and long-term Internet-based activities or projects provide individual learning opportunities that are tailored for students' growth and academic achievement. Brain-compatible Internet projects provide students with choices, meaningful context, and valuable interactive learning time, helping students make sense of the information they are learning. As students work on individual projects, teachers have time to give immediate feedback on an individual basis, thus reducing the students' natural fear of failure.

Because using the Internet usually requires individuals or small groups to work independently, teachers need to instruct students in the skills of independent work habits. Without the ability to work independently, students reduce the learning and engagement inherent in Internet activities and may become thorns in their teacher's side. The ability to work alone results from intrapersonal intelligence, and teachers can discuss the importance of self-monitoring within this important intelligence area. Teachers can help students strengthen

Multiple Intelligences and Internet Opportunities	
Intelligence	**Internet Opportunities**
Verbal/Linguistic	e-mail, chat rooms, Listserv, newsgroups, access to libraries, online journals, e-zines, electronic publishing, bulletin boards, and text used in most sites
Logical/Mathematical	databases, current research, information and data analysis, math and science game sites, scientific simulations, and sequential problem-solving opportunities
Visual/Spatial	virtual tours of museums around the world, virtual reality sites, video bits, three-dimensional representations, clip art, colorful displays, and graphic environments
Bodily/Kinesthetic	centers for health and research, information on athletics and dancing, manipulation skills used for basic keyboarding and games
Musical/Rhythmic	sites highlighting music genres and history, downloading music, sound files in some sites
Interpersonal	telementoring, online discussion groups, travelers' guides, keypals, e-mail communications, working with others on Internet projects
Intrapersonal	personal home pages, personal thoughts and reflections expressed in e-mail, Listserv, and discussion groups.
Naturalist	electronic field trips, geographical sites, environmental and social action sites

Figure 2.3

their independent work habits and increase their motivation by setting timelines for the completion of work, by teaching students to self-edit their work, and by taking time to instruct students on how to present their work creatively and professionally. This last point is especially important. Students must be taught—directly and in concrete terms—what an excellent final product includes and what it looks like. Students need to see, experience, and read good examples of final products. By providing these examples, teachers help students set goals for themselves and greatly enhance their quality of work.

When a teacher provides class time for students to work on Internet projects, he or she must set expectations for behavior. Without expectations and appropriate follow-through, independent work on Internet projects simply will not succeed. The opportunity to develop one of the most important skills students need to learn for today's world—the ability to motivate themselves to complete an independent project—may fall by the wayside. Teachers can set simple expectations: work quietly, be sensitive to others' work habits, ask a peer for help before asking an adult, and visit only Internet sites specified in the activity or allowed by the teacher.

Designing Learning Activities to Reach Goals

This book focuses on designing activities that use brain-compatible learning principles, the multiple intelligences, the Understanding by Design framework, and the Internet. Designing Internet-based activities is a much more complex process than simply jumping into an engaging Internet project. Engagement must go hand in hand with effectiveness, ensuring that activities are tied to learning and understanding goals and to chosen assessment measures.

Learning activities can be built around projects, problems, and real-life issues to provide what the brain seeks—connections, patterns, and chunks of information that fit together (Caine & Caine, 1991). Teachers need to focus on activities that incorporate the Internet, brain-compatible learning principles, and multiple intelligences theory to help build powerful and authentic learning activities that foster these connections.

The purpose of this chapter was to lay a foundation of information theory and instructional methods for teachers to apply as they design powerful Internet-based lessons. As teachers learn to keep in mind brain-compatible learning principles, the theory of multiple intelligences, and the Understanding by Design framework, their lessons will have greater depth and more significance in the lives of their students. The next chapter looks at the practical details of designing Internet-based lessons with these thoughts in mind.

3

Assessing Internet-Based Activities

ASSESSMENT: THE GREAT DEBATE

Assessment should not and cannot be polarized. It is that simple. Many educators spend hours arguing the benefits of standardized testing over authentic assessments or vice versa. Some educators who strongly believe in the theory of multiple intelligences write and speak out against the evils of standardized testing—asserting that it serves no student and actually harms some who consistently fail.

Because students do not come in nice, neat, little packages, it is important to recognize that assessments also do not come in nice, neat, little packages. The goal of assessment is to provide a photo album of a student's achievement and growth. One snapshot might be a standardized test score, another a classroom exam, and still another an Internet-based project. A myriad of photos compose this photo album. By continuing to create and analyze more photos, teachers, parents, and students begin to see where the child has grown and where he or she needs to put in more work.

There are two major criticisms of standardized testing. The first is that it focuses on what students do not know—commonly referred to as deficit-based testing. The second is that standardized tests assess only students' verbal and linguistic and logical and mathematical intelligences. In spite of these drawbacks, standardized testing does have a role and purpose for students, parents, and teachers. It provides a yardstick that can be used for all students and provides valuable information about how a student's achievement compares to his or her peers. By finding out what a particular student does not know, a teacher can determine how to work with the student in regards to a specific verbal and linguistic or logical and mathematical skill.

Yet *testing* is not a synonym for *assessment*. Standardized testing must be balanced by authentic assessment measures. Classroom projects focusing on what students know and can do, portfolios displaying students' selected work samples, and Internet-based projects and products reflecting students' developing multiple intelligences round out the photo album. These authentic assessment products should display a wide range of multiple intelligences, provide students with an opportunity to show their areas of strengths, and allow students to be recognized for what they can do well. In other words, students can demonstrate their understanding and mastery of a domain of study in multiple ways.

These authentic assessment measures also illuminate areas where students need further instruction and practice. Teachers, who are skilled in studying and analyzing student work, quickly recognize the power of using authentic student work to identify where students need further assistance and instruction. In doing this, assessment is closely and directly linked to instruction and is not an island unto itself. Assessment affects the delivery of instruction just as instructional methods influence the type of assessment used.

By providing ongoing formal and informal assessments, teachers can evaluate if their students are gaining understanding or forming misunderstandings. As teachers spend more time thinking like assessors and not just activity designers, several key questions emerge.

- What evidence indicates that students understand the material?
- What performance tasks help focus the instruction for students?
- What distinguishes students who really understand from those who do not?

For teachers grappling with creating assessments that measure understanding, Wiggins and McTighe's (1998/2005) matrix (shown in Figure 3.1) matches assessment types to the three levels of knowledge discussed in Chapter 1. This figure shows the commonly used assessment methods for each achievement level. Because all three levels are taught throughout any given day, the assessment methods must vary to achieve a balanced photo album of assessment. Of course, most teachers quickly recognize that they want students to gain understanding more than they want them simply to become familiar with concepts and ideas. Therefore, performance task assessment measures take on greater importance. Teaching with multiple intelligences and the Internet assist in this critical area.

PERFORMANCE TASKS: SIX FACETS OF UNDERSTANDING RUBRICS

A further look at performance tasks is worthwhile. Students who understand concepts go beyond simply retrieving information or retelling facts and dates. Students who understand concepts know how to use the information, rather than just store the information in the card catalogs of their brains. According to Bloom's taxonomy (1956), students show understanding when they evaluate, synthesize, analyze, and apply what they have learned.

For many teachers, students show they understand when they explain a concept in their own words, using their own thoughts. Students who understand

Matching Achievement Target and Assessment Method	
Achievement Target	**Assessment Method Most Commonly Used**
Level 1: Knowledge worth being familiar with	Standardized tests; traditional quizzes and tests: paper-and-pencil exams, constructed response
Level 2: Knowledge and skills important to know and do	Traditional quizzes and tests: paper-and-pencil exams, constructed response; performance tasks and projects with complex, open-ended, and authentic activities
Level 3: Enduring understanding	Performance tasks and projects with complex, open-ended, and authentic activities

Figure 3.1

concepts use original analogies and generalizations and apply their knowledge to make a product or complete a project that demonstrates this deep learning.

In *What Works in Schools: Translating Research Into Action,* Robert Marzano (2003) writes that "learning requires multiple exposure to and complex interactions with knowledge" (p. 112).

If a student does not receive enough exposures and interactions with knowledge, the consequence can be the inability to apply his or her understanding of the knowledge or skills to a new situation or problem. If an individual cannot do this, he or she really does not have true understanding. Students can fake understanding in a classroom setting by giving well-stored information back to teachers at the right time. Yet when out on their own, these students are unable to transfer their knowledge to new situations, leaving them in the gray area beyond knowledge acquisition but not yet at the level of achieving a deep understanding.

Although standardized tests and classroom-based quizzes and assessments have a role in student assessment, they rarely move beyond asking students to simply retrieve and return facts and pieces of information. Standardized tests and other similar assessment measures are very capable and designed to assess students' knowledge at the first two levels: knowledge worth being familiar with and knowledge and skills students should know and be able to do. When teachers move beyond these two levels and seek to assess students' understanding, other types of assessment measures must be used. These assessments measure students' ability to apply knowledge to solving problems or creating products in real-life situations. When students do this, teachers literally observe their students' understanding of what they have learned.

During a symposium on teaching for understanding, Stone Wiske (1998) from Harvard University stated that for teachers to assess students' understanding, assessment must

1. be based on relevant, explicit criteria;
2. be conducted frequently;
3. use multiple sources;

4. include a variety of forms; and
5. gauge progress and inform instruction.

Wiggins and McTighe (1998/2005) address the first of these criteria by developing six facets of understanding as potential evidence that teachers can use to evaluate student understanding. These six facets not only assist in developing learning activities but also provide a framework for assessing students' understandings (see Figure 3.2).

After examining the six facets in light of assessment, teachers can use a simplified Understanding Assessment Form (see Figure 3.3) to provide evaluation and feedback to students after they have completed an activity or project. (*Note:* A copy of Figure 3.3 can also be found in Appendix B.)

Assessments, such as the Understanding Assessment Form, should not come as a surprise to students. Teachers should give this assessment form to students before any learning activity. That way, students begin and complete a project or activity with a clear understanding of how and what they need to show and do to demonstrate understanding. Although more complex rubric forms based on the six facets appear in later sections of this chapter, the Understanding Assessment Form should be used for activities that call for a simple and quick assessment form that students are familiar with.

RUBRICS

When assessing whether students have retained specific information, evaluation often focuses on answering questions with right or wrong answers. Students either know the answer, or they do not. Yet when seeking to assess understanding, teachers quickly realize that understanding is not a matter of right versus wrong—the majority of the time understanding falls along a continuum. Understanding can easily drop through the cracks of testing and grading because it is easier to measure right versus wrong answers than it is to determine where the student falls on the continuum of understanding a specific subject or concept.

One strategy that can be used to assess understanding is the use of rubrics. A rubric is the written criteria—or guide—by which student performance or a student product is judged. Rubrics help students become active participants in their learning. They ask students to take responsibility for their own learning, growth, and achievement. Good rubrics are clear and concise—stating up front what students need to be able to know and be able to do to be successful. Well-designed rubrics provide a goal for students to reach and lay out a vision of a well-done project or activity. In his book, *Results: The Key to Continuous School Improvement,* Schmoker (1999) identified three benefits that result from using rubrics in assessing student learning and understanding:

1. Rubrics promote good performance by clearly defining that performance and by showing that such work is achievable.
2. Rubrics provide better feedback than the current system by requiring more precision and clarity about criteria for evaluation of student work.

Facets of Understanding and Assessment	
Facet of Understanding	**Assessment Glance**
Explanation: An ability to explain ideas and concepts using knowledgeable accounts of events and ideas	• Students make sophisticated or complex explanations of events or ideas. • Students go beyond given information to make inferences and connections in their explanations. • Students justify their explanations and opinions using knowledge and information.
Interpretation: An ability to make an interpretation of events or ideas and describe an event's significance and importance	• Students use storytelling and other methods to make their interpretations of knowledge and information come alive. • Students define the meaning of a story or event based on their own knowledge and opinions, not just those of others.
Application: An ability to use knowledge effectively in new and diverse situations (i.e., the ability to actually use the information and understanding in new ways)	• Students apply what they have learned and transfer their understanding into other areas and projects. • Students use information to solve new and different types of problems, thus showing understanding.
Perspective: An ability to form critical and insightful points of view, perceive things from an objective point of view, and recognize that multiple perspectives exist for any complex issue	• Students recognize that a problem or issue can be seen in multiple perspectives and that many times there is no one right answer. • Students expose unexamined assumptions and conclusions and ask critical questions.
Empathy: An ability to understand another person's feelings and perceptions, to walk in another's shoes, and to grasp another's emotional reactions and reality	• Students put aside their own feelings and opinions and learn to see and feel what others are experiencing or have experienced. • Students see actions and events through others' eyes and even change their opinions based on this experience. (*Note:* Empathy is a major foundation of the interpersonal intelligence.)
Self-Knowledge: An ability to recognize what one knows and does not know and how one's patterns of thought and action inform as well as hinder understanding	• Students understand their own thoughts, feelings, and emotions, and how those things relate to their understanding of the world. (*Note:* This is intrapersonal intelligence at its best.)

Figure 3.2

Source: Adapted with Permission from *Understanding by Design* by Wiggins, Grant and McTighe, Jay. Alexandria, VA: ASCD, 1998, pp. 9–10, 14–16, 27, 31, 76–77.

3. Rubrics bring an end to students' disheartening experience of handing in work without really knowing how the teacher will evaluate it and with no idea of whether the teacher will think it is excellent or shoddy. (p. 79)

Understanding Assessment Form Scale: 1 = does not display ability in work to 5 = displays ability throughout work, showing an understanding of concepts and ideas		
Facet of Understanding	**Explanation of Understanding**	**Assessment Rubric and Comments**
Explanation	An ability to explain ideas and concepts using knowledgeable accounts of events and ideas	1 2 3 4 5 Comments:
Interpretation	An ability to make an interpretation of events and ideas and describe an event's significance and importance	1 2 3 4 5 Comments:
Application	An ability to use knowledge effectively in new and diverse situations (i.e., the ability to use the information and understanding in new ways)	1 2 3 4 5 Comments:
Perspective	An ability to form critical and insightful points of view, perceive things from an objective point of view, and recognize that multiple perspectives exist for any complex issue	1 2 3 4 5 Comments:
Empathy	The ability to understand another person's feelings and perceptions, to walk in another's shoes, and to grasp another's emotional reactions and reality	1 2 3 4 5 Comments:
Self-Knowledge	The ability to recognize what one knows and does not know and how one's patterns of thought and action inform as well as hinder understanding	1 2 3 4 5 Comments:

Figure 3.3

Source: Adapted with Permission from *Understanding by Design* by Wiggins, Grant and McTighe, Jay. Alexandria, VA: ASCD, 1998, pp. 9–10, 14–16, 27, 31, 76–77.

Another large benefit of using rubrics comes from how easily and powerfully rubrics can be correlated to standards. Because more and more states are creating grade-level and content-area standards, rubrics provide an avenue for teachers to link these standards to assessment and instruction, ensuring that students become familiar with and learn each specific standard. In fact, performance-based assessments that are designed with standards in mind guarantee that any extra time teachers put into the development of these assessments is time well spent because it is time aimed at a specific goal and standard that needs to be taught.

In using rubrics to assess student understanding, teachers can also create rubrics that relate to the multiple intelligences and Internet activities that are a part of the overall project and learning experience. Teachers must remember that the intelligences do not work in isolation—for most individuals, the intelligences work together in a fairly well-organized way. However, if a teacher wants to focus on a specific intelligence, it is possible to create a rubric that directly relates to that intelligence. The teacher either assesses how well a student performed within that single intelligence or how well a student understands the content of what was being taught by using that single intelligence as a vehicle in his or her learning experience. Most likely there will be a time and place for both types of assessment. Teachers can easily create rubrics that assess students' understanding of a concept and, in the next activity, use a rubric that evaluates students' mastery of a specific intelligence as shown in the complexity of the end product. It is also possible for teachers to use rubrics to assess how well students are progressing along the continuum of skills and knowledge in their use of the Internet. Teachers may also choose to create a series of rubrics using the multiple intelligences based on what is being taught and learned in their classrooms.

Rules for the Rubric Road

The following guidelines are useful for teachers when developing rubrics:

1. Keep rubrics as simple and clear as possible. Write rubrics in language that students can understand and refer to throughout the project.
2. Continually review the rubric with students. This keeps the expectations for student work clearly defined and known.
3. Create rubrics that deal with big picture assessments. Avoid overwhelming students with a rubric for each activity. Use rubrics across domains and activities to help students focus on the skills needed to drive them toward mastery and understanding.
4. When possible, involve students in the development of the rubric. This helps them feel empowered and assisted through the assessment process.
5. Clearly communicate the rubric to parents. If they understand the rubric, parents can assist their child in creating a product that works with it.
6. Attach the rubric to the students' work. This gives direct feedback regarding the submitted work.

Understanding Rubrics: Assessing the Complete Package

Figure 3.4 shows a rubric based on the six facets of understanding and is expanded to include multiple intelligences and Internet skills. (*Note:* A blank copy of the rubric is included in Appendix B.) This rubric is a simplified version of the one presented in Wiggins and McTighe's book, *Understanding by Design* (1998/2005), and has been adapted to include the Internet and the theory of multiple intelligences. Teachers can use this rubric to assess any of the Internet projects presented in this book. Figure 3.5 gives an example of using the form to assess a student's work.

Information Literacy Rubric

Information literacy relates to the skills that support finding, evaluating, and using information, and, for this book, have a focus on electronic-based information sources. Because these skills are critical to successful Internet-based activities, they are discussed in more detail in Chapter 5. To help teachers plan for assessing these skills, an information literacy rubric is presented next.

Teachers who are consistently reinforcing the information literacy skills may find the rubric shown in Figure 3.6 useful. (*Note:* A blank copy of the rubric is included in Appendix B.) This rubric can be applied to specific research assignments when students work with large amounts of information. It is helpful for students to receive feedback on how their information literacy skills are progressing throughout the year. This rubric keeps these skills in the forefront of students' minds as they work on a project.

Multiple Intelligences Rubric: Assessment Measures

Gardner (1993) supported the notion that in order to assess students' understandings, students must be able to complete "performances of understanding" or what are more commonly referred to as performance-based assessment measures. Simply put, students must be able to show their understanding in a variety of ways. Using and assessing multiple intelligences allows students to do this. When students use their verbal and linguistic intelligence to write five-paragraph essays about a subject, they do not necessarily ensure that they have a deep and genuine understanding of the topic. Teachers can ensure understanding by requiring multiple representations of students learning using the different intelligence areas.

Designing Internet-based activities that use multiple intelligences allows students to show multiple representations of learning. Figure 3.7 provides a list of Internet and other technological products that can serve as assessment measures or performances of understanding.

By observing and providing feedback to students regarding their different intelligences, teachers heighten students' awareness of their intelligence strengths and weaknesses. Teachers can easily provide ongoing feedback by attaching a multiple intelligences rubric form to the project as part of its evaluation criteria. Figure 3.8 is a sample description of the rubric components. (*Note:* A blank copy of the rubric is included in Appendix B.)

Teachers may use a Generalized Multiple Intelligences Rubric when looking at how students use their multiple intelligences and provide ongoing feedback to students about these observations. This type of feedback is valuable to increase students' awareness of the different intelligences and to recognize students' efforts to use a variety of intelligences in their work.

The Generalized Multiple Intelligences Rubric provides an overview of some activities and skills that might be considered masterful, skilled, and basic in each intelligence area. However, there are times when a teacher may want to

Understanding Rubric			
Facet of Understanding	**Masterful (3)**	**Skilled (2)**	**Basic (1)**
Explanation	• Gives a thorough and inventive explanation that is fully supported.	• Gives an explanation that reflects some in-depth ideas but needs more evidence.	• Gives a superficial explanation that is more descriptive than analytical.
Interpretation	• Gives a powerful interpretation and analysis of the meaning and importance of the subject matter.	• Gives a plausible interpretation of the subject matter. • Makes sense of a story and provides a useful history or context of the story.	• Gives a simple and superficial interpretation of subject matter. • Student does not understand significance.
Application	• Applies knowledge and understanding with fluency and flexibility. • Able to apply in novel situations. • Uses a variety of multiple intelligences in activity.	• Performs well with knowledge in a limited way. • Relies on routine and familiar contexts to help with application.	• Only applies knowledge with help from teacher or others or by relying on clearly laid out skills and procedures.
Perspective	• Expresses a revealing and novel viewpoint. • Considers others' perspectives.	• Uses a reasonably critical and comprehensive look at all points of view.	• Appears unaware of differing points of view. • Has difficulty imagining other ways of perceiving things.
Empathy	• Sees and feels what others are experiencing; open to the unfamiliar or different. • Demonstrates strong interpersonal intelligence skills.	• Knows and feels what others see and feel, but may still be limited to one's own reactions and puzzled by the unfamiliar.	• Has little empathy beyond intellectual awareness of others. • Ignores or is puzzled by others' different views.
Self-Knowledge	• Deeply aware of the boundaries of one's own understanding and able to	• Generally aware of what is and is not understood yet unaware of how	• Generally aware of one's own ignorance yet does not understand the

(Continued)

Understanding Rubric (Continued)			
Facet of Understanding	**Masterful (3)**	**Skilled (2)**	**Basic (1)**
	recognize one's own prejudices. • Possesses strong intrapersonal intelligence.	prejudgments can color understandings.	role of prejudice or prejudgments.
Internet Skills	• Follows directions independently and participates in Internet activity with little or no guidance. • Understands the Internet's role in activity. • Focuses on the Internet as a tool within the learning activity and not as an end to itself.	• Follows directions with minor guidance and assistance. • Uses the Internet to learn curriculum topic but continues to refine Internet skills to make this learning smoother.	• Requires consistent help in using the Internet and is unable to participate in the activity without breaking the flow to ask for help. • Focuses on the Internet procedures more than the curriculum activity.
Use of Multiple Intelligences	• Uses a variety of intelligences in a complex and thoughtful way. • Able to articulate what intelligences are being used and why each was necessary for success of project.	• Uses a variety of intelligences yet is unaware of the roles each plays in the project's success. • Needs guidance in the use of one or two intelligences.	• Uses one or two intelligences in a basic and simplistic fashion. • Unaware of the use of different intelligences. • Needs repeated guidance and assistance in all intelligences.

Figure 3.4

isolate specific intelligences and assess how students are progressing along the continuum of strengthening each intelligence area. The intelligences very rarely work in isolation, so teachers must not place too much emphasis on attempting to isolate and evaluate each student's different intelligences.

Teachers can tweak the Generalized Multiple Intelligences Rubric to fit activities and their own style of teaching and learning. For example, a teacher may develop a multiple intelligences rubric for a unit on fractions that he or she teaches each year. To begin, this teacher would examine how he or she wants students to use their different intelligences within this unit and then create clear, concise examples and criteria for each intelligence that will be focused on. This type of rubric usually includes only a few of the intelligences.

(Continued on bottom of page 45.)

Understanding Rubric Example

Name: Mary
Rubric for: Electronic Publishing Activity

Score: 15 of 24
Grade: C+

Facet of Understanding	Masterful (3)	Skilled (2)	Basic (1)
Explanation		Mary was able to explain her nonfiction story with clarity yet needed more examples and in-depth ideas.	
Interpretation	Mary provided an excellent interpretation of her historical event. Understood importance of events.		
Application		Mary wrote her story using independent work habits yet required ongoing adult supervision.	
Perspective			Mary struggled to understand the different perspectives of the historical event.
Empathy		Mary showed great empathy for those involved in the event, yet was puzzled by others' feelings.	
Self-Knowledge		Mary is aware that she feels indifferent toward important events, yet she is unaware of how this affects writing.	
Internet Skills		Mary accessed electronic publishing site quickly, yet was unable to independently submit her story to site.	
Use of Multiple Intelligences			Mary showed some use of verbal/linguistic skills yet did not use interpersonal intelligence.

Figure 3.5

Information Literacy Skills Rubric			
Information	**Masterful (3)**	**Skilled (2)**	**Basic (1)**
1. Know when there is a need for information. (Comprehension)	• Recognizes when there is a need for information to solve a problem or develop an idea. • Brainstorms multiple strategies for approaching the identified problem or issue. • Identifies, organizes, and sequences tasks to complete an information-based project.	• Aware that there is a need for information. • Identifies one or two strategies for approaching the problem. • Identifies the tasks to complete the project. • Struggles to stay organized through the sequence of task completion.	• Unaware of a need for information to solve a problem. • After need is pointed out, develops a simplified strategy for approaching the problem. • Has trouble identifying and sequencing tasks to complete the project.
2. Find and identify the information needed. (Comprehension and Analysis)	• Formulates questions based on information needs. • Uses effective search techniques. • Analyzes various sources for relevance. • Reads competently to understand the information presented.	• Formulates simplistic questions based on information needs. • Uses effective search techniques. • Does not analyze sources for relevance.	• Forms questions with assistance. • Cannot search for information independently. • Does not analyze sources for relevance.
3. Analyze the information. (Analysis and Evaluation)	• Evaluates the quality of information by establishing authority. • Determines accuracy and authenticity. • Distinguishes among opinion, reasoned arguments, and fact.	• Evaluates the quality of information independently. • Does not establish authority • Is aware of the difference between opinion, argument, and fact, yet has trouble distinguishing differences.	• Evaluates the quality of information with assistance and using a simplified evaluation. • Does not yet establish authority. • Vaguely aware of differences between opinion, argument, and fact.
4. Organize the information. (Application)	• Knows how knowledge is organized.	• Organizes information in a searchable format.	• Struggles to organize information in searchable formats.

Information Literacy Skills Rubric (Continued)			
Information	**Masterful (3)**	**Skilled (2)**	**Basic (1)**
	• Organizes and stores data in searchable formats. • Organizes information for practical application.	• Needs to continue to strengthen abilities to organize it for practical application.	• Uses a simplified organization structure that makes sense to them.
5. Use the information effectively to address the problem or task. (Synthesis)	• Creates new information by synthesizing data from primary and secondary sources. • Integrates new information to existing knowledge. • Summarizes information found in sources.	• Creates new information in a simplified format based on synthesizing data. • Integrates new information into existing knowledge. • Struggles to provide a thorough summary of information.	• Struggles to create new information. • Integrates new information into existing knowledge base. • Summarizes information with assistance.
6. Communicate the information and evaluate the results. (Application and Evaluation)	• Presents information in a product form. • Documents sources using appropriate formats. • Performs ongoing evaluation by revising and updating the product.	• Presents information in a product form and documents sources. • Product is well done yet could be more complex and detailed. • Revises and updates product regularly.	• Presents information in a simplified product form. • Does not document sources using appropriate formats. • Does not revise or update product independently.

Figure 3.6

Source: Adapted from "Computer Skills for Information Problem Solving: Learning and Teaching Technology in Context" by M. B. Eisenberg and D. Johnson. *ERIC Digest:* March, 1996. (ED392463)

For example, a fractions unit might focus on the verbal and linguistic, music and rhythmic, and logical and mathematical intelligences as shown in Figure 3.9.

After teachers discover how easy it is to modify the Generalized Multiple Intelligence Rubric (Figure 3.8) to develop personalized rubrics for different curricular areas, they can create and collect well-designed rubrics to use again and again. An example of a modified rubric for a curriculum area is Figure 3.9, which provides a rubric for a fraction unit that includes the multiple intelligences. The

Multiple Intelligences and Technology Assessment Menu			
Verbal/ Linguistic	**Logical/ Mathematical**	**Visual/ Spatial**	**Bodily/ Kinesthetic**
• Essay/narrative writing • Electronic publishing products • E-mail correspondences • Electronic learning log or journal • Posters or brochures	• Spatial or graphic organizers • Logical analysis and critique • Pattern games and sites • Annotated outlines • Database projects • Data analysis products	• Design of Web site • Graphic representations of information • Reading and creating maps • Flowcharts and graphs • Mind maps • Video recording and photography on Internet	• Impersonations • Showing physical representation, role play, tableau of something learned via Internet • Research project via Internet on sports, drama, etc.
Musical/ Rhythmic	**Interpersonal**	**Intrapersonal**	**Naturalist**
• Creating and publishing original music • Composing music • Analyzing musical structure • Reproducing musical patterns	• Teach others via Internet • E-mail • Keypals • Question and answer discussions with others • Electronic surveys and questionnaires • Telementoring learning	• Metacognitive surveys • Electronic journals • electronic autobiography • Social action project (students interact on personally important issues)	• Species and natural pattern classification • Care for plants and animals • Conservation practices and knowledge • Virtual field trips

Figure 3.7

more these rubrics are used, the more awareness students will gain as they use and strengthen their different intelligences.

Internet Skills Rubric

Along the same vein as rubrics to accommodate multiple intelligences in instruction, rubrics can also be designed to assess Internet skills. Because students need to master Internet skills and strategies, it is helpful for teachers to provide feedback to them regarding their progression along the continuum of these valuable skills. Teachers should directly teach and discuss these types of skills so that students are aware of them throughout their Internet projects.

(Continued on bottom of page 49.)

Generalized Multiple Intelligences Rubric			
Intelligence	**Masterful (3)**	**Skilled (2)**	**Basic (1)**
Verbal/Linguistic	• Creates original stories and executes various types of formal writing and speaking. • Engages in metalinguistic analysis.	• Properly uses language to communicate ideas. • Uses written communication to express feelings and opinions; shows comprehension of information.	• Displays knowledge of the alphabet and use of written and oral language in simplistic forms. • Performs simple writing tasks when provided assistance.
Logical/Mathematical	• Links various math operations for complex problem solving. • Engages in both inductive and deductive reasoning.	• Performs a range of standard math operations and calculations. • Grasps a variety of problem-solving skills; engages in abstract thinking and logic	• Performs concrete object manipulations and counts. • Performs basic sequencing tasks. • Recognizes simple concrete cause and effect relationships.
Visual/Spatial	• Makes something from a pattern. • Shows accurate mapmaking skills. • Creates impressionistic art forms. • Displays understanding of abstract spatial images.	• Reproduces spatial depth, scenes, and objects through drawing and painting. • Understands reading maps. • Displays an active imagination and recognizes objects from different perspectives.	• Enjoys a variety of colors, shapes, images, and designs. • Creates simple drawings. • Manipulates objects to assemble simple creations.
Musical/Rhythmic	• Uses music and rhythm to express ideas and to create and share music with others. • Understands different musical forms and the language of music.	• Produces different kinds of melodies and shows an awareness of the impact of various kinds of music. • Matches music with one's feelings and enjoys a variety of music.	• Recognizes and responds to different tones. • Reproduces a variety of sounds and patterns. • Associates emotions with different pieces of music.

(Continued)

Generalized Multiple Intelligences Rubric (Continued)			
Intelligence	**Masterful (3)**	**Skilled (2)**	**Basic (1)**
Bodily/Kinesthetic	• Performs in a variety of creative activities and uses body movements to express feelings and thoughts. • Executes complex physical movements.	• Uses a variety of expressive gestures and body language. • Has a strongly developed sense of coordinated motor skills. • Shows success in hands-on creations.	• Participates in various automatic physical reflexes and performs simple motor skills. • Begins to use actions to achieve control over environment.
Interpersonal	• Builds consensus in a group and manages conflict between others. • Understands group dynamics. • Is sensitive to individual differences and opinions.	• Builds meaningful peer relationships and has effective social skills. • Empathizes with others. • Is an effective member of a team or group.	• Establishes meaningful relationships with family members. • Uses simple communication skills with others.
Intrapersonal	• Expresses oneself through various strategies. • Controls own emotions and moods. • Explores personal feelings. • Easily participates in metacognitive analyses.	• Develops an appreciation of individual uniqueness. • Defines and understands own likes and dislikes. • Understands how one's behavior affects other relationships.	• Aware of and expresses a variety of feelings and moods. • Recognizes different emotional states and tries to make sense of one's own behavior and feelings.
Naturalist	• Discerns new patterns and connections between the natural and human worlds. • Participates in creative experiments to test own ideas about nature. • Senses subtle connections between environment and own self.	• Makes observations that raise questions and thoughts. • Makes connections between sounds, smells, and sights from the environment. • Sees unusual patterns that are not obvious and can create categories. • Uses nature in creative ways.	• Uses items from the environment to identify obvious patterns and connections in nature. • Responds to obvious input from environment and reproduces experiments already performed.

Figure 3.8

Multiple Intelligences Rubric Adapted for a Fractions Unit			
Intelligence	**Masterful (3)**	**Skilled (2)**	**Basic (1)**
Verbal/Linguistic	• Creates original fraction story and uses personification in the explanation of a complex concept. • Shows understanding of how fractions work through written description and story about fractions.	• Writes a story about fractions and gives different fractions a personality and character. • Uses story line to teach fraction concept. • Shows comprehension of information.	• Orally tells a story using fractions as characters yet is unable to show understanding of the math concept being taught.
Logical/Mathematical	• Uses mathematical and computational skills to understand and work with fractions.	• Uses mathematical skills to work with fractions yet struggles to understand concepts.	• Struggles to use mathematical skills to work with fractions. • Shows difficulty in understanding fraction concepts.
Musical/Rhythmic	• Uses music and rhythm to demonstrate ideas and knowledge about fractions. • Understands different musical forms and how fractions influence rhythm.	• Produces different kinds of melodies. • Is aware of the impact fractions have on various kinds of music.	• Recognizes and responds to fractions as being a part of music yet is unable to explain the concept or use fractions in a musical demonstration.

Figure 3.9

The rubric in Figure 3.10 is a simple Internet skills assessment tool that can be attached to any product or activity when students use the Internet. (*Note:* A blank copy of the rubric is included in Appendix B.)

Just as there are multiple intelligences, there are multiple ways of assessing student skills and levels of understanding. Through using rubrics, performance-based assessments, classroom tests and assignments, standardized tests, or projects, teachers can create strong assessment programs that are ongoing, include a variety of assessments, and are directly linked to what students are learning and being taught. As teachers demystify the assessment process for students, they can use assessment as an instructional strategy to guide student learning and to motivate students to achieve at higher levels.

Internet Skills Rubric			
Internet Skill	**Masterful (3)**	**Skilled (2)**	**Basic (1)**
Search Engines	• Uses search engines to find information. • Employs searching techniques to make searches more effective.	• Recognizes the importance and use of search engines yet is not fully efficient in using techniques to make searches more effective.	• Recognizes what search engines are yet struggles in using techniques to find information.
E-mail	• Uses e-mail to communicate well with others. • Derives information from e-mail communications.	• Communicates effectively with others via e-mail. • Is unaware of the ability to gain information from e-mail communications.	• Is aware of what e-mail is yet does not use it to communicate well with others. • Struggles in writing e-mail to others.
Bookmarks and Folders	• Uses bookmarks and folders effectively to store and organize information. • Is aware of the importance of organizing Internet information.	• Is aware of what bookmarks and folders are and their importance yet struggles in using them efficiently.	• Is unaware of the purpose and role of bookmarks and folders. • Does not use them in Internet work.
Links	• Knows how to follow links and maneuver around Web pages to find information. • Is able to follow links back to original starting point.	• Is able to follow links in Web sites yet struggles to regain a sense of sequence and order in traveling through the links.	• Gets easily confused in using links in different Web sites. • Struggles to stay on task in Internet work due to misunderstanding links.
Internet Technology	• Understands major Internet terms. • Is able to use terms in a meaningful way that shows understanding.	• Recognizes most major Internet terms. • Uses terms in a simplistic way that shows basic comprehension yet lacks understanding.	• Struggles to understand major Internet terms. • Shows confusion over terminology.

Internet Skills Rubric (Continued)			
Internet Skill	**Masterful (3)**	**Skilled (2)**	**Basic (1)**
Download Files	• Knows how to download files from the Internet to save on the hard drive. • Is able to help others in downloading files.	• Knows how to download files from Internet yet struggles in helping others do the same.	• Struggles to understand the process of downloading files from the Internet.
E-mail Etiquette	• Is aware of e-mail etiquette on a regular basis. • Recognizes what the etiquette comprises and why it is important.	• Uses e-mail etiquette in communications on an inconsistent basis. • Does not grasp the purpose of such etiquette.	• Is unaware of e-mail etiquette. • Does not use it purposely in e-mail communications.
Web Site Evaluation	• Is able to evaluate Web sites for authenticity and facts. • Is able to look beyond the appearance of the site in evaluation.	• Evaluates Web sites for content and appearance yet struggles with authenticity and facts.	• Struggles to get past the appearance of the Web site in evaluation process.

Figure 3.10

4

Using the Internet to Strengthen Interpersonal Skills

After teachers understand how to use the Understanding by Design framework and the preplanning questions provided in Chapter 1 and how to create and use rubrics from Chapter 3, they can focus on designing a wide variety of Internet-based learning activities. These projects and experiences play a dual role—helping students learn and better understand concepts and curricular subjects while providing opportunities for using and strengthening their intelligences.

This chapter examines the use of interpersonal exchange activities on the Internet. Before jumping into the abyss of the Internet, it is important that teachers and students have a foundation of Internet knowledge and skills at their disposal. This foundation includes a general knowledge of the history of the Internet (a good example of knowledge worth being familiar with but not really needed for true understanding) and knowledge about search engines and making searches more productive and effective (a good example of important knowledge worth knowing).

THE HISTORY OF THE INTERNET

The origins of the Internet go back to 1957, the International Geophysical Year. This year was dedicated to gathering information about the upper atmosphere during a period of intense solar activity. In October of that year, the United Soviet Socialist Republic launched Sputnik. The effect in the United

States was electrifying because overnight it obliterated the feeling of invulnerability the United States had enjoyed since the explosion of the first nuclear bomb 13 years earlier. The United States government immediately reacted by creating the Advanced Research Projects Agency (ARPA) within the Department of Defense.

By 1966, research had advanced so far that the head of computer research, Leonard Roberts, published a plan for a computer network system called ARPANET. When these plans were published, it was discovered that teams at the Massachusetts Institute of Technology (MIT), the National Physics Laboratory (in the United Kingdom), and the RAND Corporation had all been working independently on having computers in different locations communicate with one another. Their best ideas were incorporated into the ARPANET design.

Next, a protocol was determined to allow computers to send and receive messages and data, known as an interface message processor (IMP). Work on an IMP was completed in 1968, and the time was right to test the theory.

In October 1969, using computers at both the University of California at Los Angeles (UCLA) and Stanford University, UCLA students were able to log in to Stanford's computer, access its databases, and send basic data. The experiment was successful, and the first network had come into being. By December 1969, ARPANET comprised four host computers with the addition of research centers in Santa Barbara, California, and Utah. The first true computer network was born.

In October 1972, ARPANET went public. At the First International Conference on Computers and Communication, scientists demonstrated the system in operation, linking computers together from 40 different locations. This stimulated further research in scientific communities throughout the Western world. Other networks soon began to appear.

In 1972, a new program was employed to send messages over the Internet, allowing direct person-to-person communication—now referred to as e-mail. In 1974, ARPA scientists developed a common language that allowed different networks to communicate with each other. This was known as a Transmission Control Protocol/Internet Protocol (TCP/IP).

This sharing of design information was an integral part of the research environment and greatly facilitated subsequent technological advances. At this stage, the world almost exclusively used large mainframe computers owned only by large corporations, government institutions, and universities. The system, therefore, was designed with the expectation that it would work through a limited number of national networks.

Although 1974 marked the beginning of TCP/IP, it would take several years of modification and redesign before the protocol was completed and universally adopted. For example, one adaptation designed in the mid-1970s was a stripped-down version that could be incorporated into the newly created microcomputers. Another design challenge was developing a version of the software that was compatible with each of the computer networks.

Until the mid-1970s, Internet development was almost entirely science led. Advances in computer capacities and speeds—and the introduction of glass-fiber cables into communications networks—were enabling the system to expand. This expansion, in its turn, produced supply constraints that stimulated further advances.

By the early 1980s, the Internet faced problems created by its own success. First, more computer hosts than had originally been envisioned were linked to the Internet. Second, the volume of traffic per host was much larger because of the phenomenal success of e-mail. Increasingly, researchers predicted that the entire system would eventually grind to a halt.

Although commercial exploitation of the Internet had started, the expansion of the Internet continued to be driven by the government and academic communities. It was also becoming ever more international. By 1989, the number of hosts surpassed 100,000 for the first time and, a year later, had climbed to 300,000. Commercial, government, and academic communities all contributed to the incredible and continuing growth of the Internet. This of course continues to grow exponentially each year.

After learning about the history of the Internet, it is time for students to learn how the Internet really works and how it can be a great asset to them on a daily basis. The following classroom activity provides students with this opportunity.

Taking It to the Classroom

What Is the Internet?

Many students when asked what the Internet is give answers that display a deep misunderstanding of what the Internet consists of and is able to do. Many students can tell what the Internet *does*—an answer usually related to finding information—yet very few understand what the Internet *is*. The basis of this lesson is to teach the concept of the Internet and some of the key terms used on the Internet. Therefore, it is a technology-oriented rather than a curriculum-oriented activity. The lesson is most appropriate for students in grades 5 to 12.

Brain-Compatibility Link

Focus Links: Collaboration, Active Learning, and Pattern Seeking

This activity consist of groups of students working together to gain knowledge and understanding of how the Internet works. This *collaboration* allows students to share ideas and reflect upon their learning of this complex technology. This activity also promotes *active learning* in the classroom. Instead of a teacher simply talking about how the Internet works and showing students a diagram, students become active participants in learning about the Internet and in constructing this knowledge themselves. Finally, part of figuring out how the Internet works consists of *seeking patterns* in this complex web of wires and communications. Students find themselves piecing together a large web of patterns that makes up this complex thing called the Internet.

Internet Terms

Bookmark: A favorite site placed in a special menu on a browser; by selecting the name, users instantaneously link to the site.

Browser: The software that allows users to work on the Internet.

Download: Transferring information from Internet to individual computers.

E-mail: Electronic mail

Home page: Document displayed when first accessing a Web site.

Internet Service Provider (ISP): Any organization or company that provides direct Internet access.

Network: People connected via computers to share information.

Server: Similar to a host, a machine that works with client systems. Servers can be personal computers or mainframes that share information with many users.

Uniform Resource Location (URL): The Internet addressing system. It may look like this: www.mywebsite.com.

Figure 4.1

Charting the Way

The preplanning questions help guide the lesson to meet goals and objectives.

Q1. What are the deep understandings of this activity?

Students gain understanding of how the Internet works.

Q2. What skills and knowledge, both academic and Internet-based, will students strengthen as a result of this activity?

Students strengthen their knowledge of the foundation of the Internet. Students strengthen Internet research skills.

Q3. What facts do students need to become familiar with through this activity?

Students gain familiarity with major Internet terms and the vocabulary used frequently on the Internet. Figure 4.1 shows nine terms about the Internet that are important for students to know. Students learn about computer connections and how different computers are connected to make the Internet run smoothly.

Q4. How can students' understanding, knowledge, and skills be assessed?

Students are assessed for their understanding of this complex issue using the Understanding Rubric (Figure 3.4 and in Appendix B). By using this rubric, teachers can assess how well students explain how the Internet works and how well they apply this knowledge with a fresh perspective, empathy, and self-knowledge. Teachers may consider having students complete a diagram explaining how the Internet works, using the appropriate Internet terms and vocabulary. The diagram should show that students understand the major concepts of the Internet infrastructure and how the different components work together.

Q5. What type of Internet activity will help students reach these learning goals? What will the Internet activity entail? How long will the activity last?

Students answer a series of questions that prompt them to visit several Internet sites to gain information about the Internet and its terminology. After students compile information, they complete the assessment activity. The project needs approximately four to five 60-minute sessions.

Q6. What intelligences can be brought into this Internet project to help students learn?

- *Verbal and Linguistic:* Students research, participate in discussion groups, read, and write.
- *Visual and Spatial:* Students draw a diagram of the Internet.
- *Interpersonal:* Students work in study groups to complete the activity and assessment piece.
- *Bodily and Kinesthetic:* If they elect to, or for extra credit, students perform a role play describing how the Internet works.

Discovering Internet-Based Resources

The following Web sites provide teachers and students with further information and additional links that relate to the Internet. These Web sites are simple and effective in explaining the Internet and how it works. Although there are hundreds of other sites available to learn about the Internet, these sites are good places to start for both teachers and students.

- Nerds 2.0.1 (www.pbs.org/opb/nerds2.0.1)
- A Brief History of the Internet (www.isoc.org/internet/history/brief.shtml)
- General Internet information at www.cyspacecity.net/support/shopsite/mgr/helpindex.internet.html

(*Note:* These and additional sites are listed in Appendix A.)

Stepping Out

Teachers use the following steps to guide the lesson process:

1. Discuss the history of the Internet to provide context.
2. Provide an overview of the activity and what students are going to learn. Tell students they will work in their designated groups to answer the question, What is the Internet? The goal of this activity is to understand what the Internet is and what it can do as well as learn some important Internet terms.
3. Discuss with students how they will be assessed by sharing the Understanding Rubric (Figure 3.4 and in Appendix B) and detailing exactly what students need to learn by the end of the activity. Tell students that they will answer a series of questions as well as create a diagram that explains how the Internet works.
4. Divide students into groups and give them the following questions to help them along on their journey of discovery. Consider asking them to answer these questions on a separate sheet of paper.
   a. Why do you think the Internet was named the Internet?
   b. Describe how computers "talk" to one another.
   c. What is e-mail and how does it work?
   d. What is a server and why is it important?
   e. What is an Internet Service Provider (ISP) and why do we all need one?
   f. What is a Uniform Resource Location (URL) and why does each Web site have one?
5. Allow students time to explore the Web sites to learn about the Internet. Ask students to create a diagram of the Internet that explains to someone else what the Internet is and how computers are connected to the Internet. Remind students that it is important that the diagram show how well they understand how the Internet works and that they keep in mind the Understanding Rubric as they work. Ask them to share their diagrams with the members of their groups and ask for feedback and constructive ideas on how to make it better.
6. Share final diagrams and discuss the questions as a class to end the activity.

SEARCHING FOR INFORMATION: SEARCH ENGINES

As the number of online users and the amount of information accessible through the Internet continued to increase, search engines were created to help people find what they were looking for in a more efficient way. There is a myriad of search engines to choose from, all of which return thousands of Web sites through very simple searches.

Not all search engines are created equal. For example, Yahoo! is considered a directory that acts very similar to a search engine. Human beings sift through thousands of Web sites each day and select sites deemed most useable for Yahoo! Search engines, such as Google and Ask, use software that acts like an electronic spider searching through Web site databases looking for the key search words. The number of sites a Google search returns is usually much higher than the number Yahoo! finds for the same search term. Yet the quality of sites may be higher on Yahoo! because people, not a software package, have selected the sites. Metasearch engines, such as Dogpile, search the top search engines all at once and return a multitude of sites to the user. Some of the most commonly used search engines include those shown in Figure 4.2.

Simplifying Searching

After discussing the concept of search engines, teachers should share with students a few handy tips for searching the Internet (see Figure 4.3). These simple suggestions quickly turn a frustrating search into a productive one. When students (and teachers) clearly specify what they want to find on the

Search Engines

Search Engine	Specialty/Target Audience
Yahoo! Kids (http://kids.yahoo.com/)	K–12 material only. Lists assembled by humans on general themes.
Yahoo! (www.yahoo.com)	Directory organized by themes. Lists assembled by humans.
Google (www.google.com)	Thorough search engine.
Google Scholar (www.scholar.google.com)	A search engine sponsored by Google that provides users access to research and written materials with a simple search.
AltaVista (www.altavista.com)	General searches. Claims to have the largest database of Web pages.
Excite (www.excite.com)	Science and math focus.
Dogpile (www.dogpile.com)	Searches the top 16 search engines. Called a metasearch engine.
HotBot (www.hotbot.com)	Specific searches.

Figure 4.2

Simple Search Rules

1. **Use the word AND when you want information about two or more keywords together.**
For example: colleges AND SAT, dolphins AND whales, Dodgers AND Giants AND Expos.

2. **Use the word NOT when you want information about one keyword, but do not want information about the other.**
For example: art NOT painting, football NOT playoffs, national parks NOT California.

3. **Use the word OR if you want sites that have at least one of the terms you are searching for.**
For example: weather OR hurricanes. This search term returns sites that have either of the terms *weather* or *hurricanes* and sites that include both. In contrast, when the search is "weather AND hurricanes" only sites that have both terms are found.

4. **Use quotation marks around the names of people, places, or a phrase.** This ensures that the words appear next to each other in the Web site. For example: "President Washington," "California beaches," "multiple intelligences theory." If the searcher does not place quotation marks around President Washington, the search engine finds any site that includes one of the words. This gives the searcher sites about the state of Washington and sites about presidents but very few sites about President Washington.

5. **To find a picture of something, type in "image:" followed by a keyword or words.**
For example: image: dog; image: Mars; image: Michael Jordan

6. **Use capital letters only if you want sites that include the search words capitalized.**
For example, if Festivals is entered, the search engine returns only sites that use the word *Festivals* and will not return sites that use the word *festivals*. By entering the term in lowercase, the searcher receives sites that use both the words *festivals* and *Festivals*.

Figure 4.3

Internet, the chances of a search engine actually finding the information is greatly enhanced. Knowing a few simple search rules helps students find the Internet a lot more friendly and efficient. Teachers should ask students to practice each search rule before working on the next rule.

As students are taught to search the Internet, many will appear quite proficient at the skill because of their home use. Yet teachers must remember that students need and want specific instruction in how to make their searches more effective. Students need to understand three points in searching the Internet:

(1) the significance of word choice, (2) the power of spelling, and (3) the value of quality over quantity.

In talking about word choice, teachers should discuss what types of keywords students need to use to find the correct information. The more specific the keyword, the more specific the returned information will be. Although this seems basic, some students need to see examples of keywords in searches.

Idea webs are one useful strategy to help students focus on the exact topic and most appropriate keyword for an effective search. Idea webs can be as simple as a mind map where students write their main idea or problem to be solved in the center of the page and make additions to the map as they think of other topics that are related. Students can then use key terms from their idea webs or mind maps as search terms.

Teachers can also demonstrate the difference between "Greek architecture" and "Geek architecture" and explain that spelling does indeed count! In fact, some search engines are sensitive to whether the query and source match on capitalization, let alone have the same letters. As minor as this point seems, it pays to remember that computers search very literally for what is entered as a query.

When discussing the value of quality over quantity in search results, teachers need to point out that getting material exactly on point is most often more useful than getting a lot of material not exactly on point. This is where good word choice pays off. On the other hand, it is a fine line sometimes between getting too much or not enough material from a search. Sometimes, to find the material in the database, the query word chosen needs to be broader or needs to be a synonym. Quality, meaning only relevant material, is the most common goal; but quantity, meaning any related material, is sometimes the necessary goal.

The following classroom activity helps students become familiar with different search engines and practice the searching techniques previously discussed.

Taking It to the Classroom

Getting to Know Search Engines

The purpose of this activity is to help students become familiar with the different types and formats of search engines. In this activity, students use the same search term(s) in several Internet searches to compare and contrast search engines. Students quickly become aware of the similarities and differences of the search engines and the variety of sites returned by different search engines. Students need to be encouraged to pay attention to the details of each search engine and to find the ones that work best for them. This activity is suitable for students in Grades 4 to 12 and assumes students possess a general understanding of search engines and have discussed searching strategies.

Brain-Compatibility Link

Focus Links: Patterns, Immediate Feedback, Repetition, and Rehearsal

This activity provides students with a study in *patterns*. Each search engine returns numerous Web sites, and it is up to students to evaluate the patterns seen in the lists of Web sites. For example, students might notice that larger Web site companies top the list on one search engine, whereas private, smaller Web sites top the list on another. As students compare search engines, patterns emerge. These patterns help students learn about the search engines and make remembering each one easier.

This activity also provides students with *immediate feedback*. They quickly receive results of their searches and can immediately analyze those results. Early in the process, students notice when they do not receive correct information from the search engines and can change their search terms as they go.

In addition, students use the same terms in numerous searches. This provides them with *repetition and rehearsal* as they learn how to use search engines effectively.

Charting the Way

The preplanning questions help guide the lesson to meet goals and objectives.

Q1. What are the deep understandings of this activity?

Students understand the complexity of Internet search engines and how they work.

Students understand how, why, and when they need to use a search engine.

Q2. What skills and knowledge, both academic and Internet-based, will students strengthen as a result of this activity?

Students learn how to work with numerous search engines.

Students learn what search engines are best for different types of information-seeking needs.

Q3. What facts do students need to become familiar with through this activity?

Students learn that there are major and minor differences among search engines.

Students learn that specific search engines are better for specific types of searches.

Q4. How can students' understanding, knowledge, and skills be assessed?

Students can be assessed based on how well they are able to complete the searches, record the information, and evaluate the search engines. Teachers look for depth and complexity of observations and comments about the types of Web sites found through each search engine. Because this is a relatively simple lesson designed to strengthen Internet skills rather than to master content, the assessment piece does not need to be as in-depth as a rubric. Instead, students should show that they have accessed the search engines and are able to compare them. If students are unable to do this, the teacher should spend time with individual students or pair students to complete the activity correctly.

Q5. What type of Internet activity will help students reach these learning goals? What will the Internet activity entail? How long will the activity last?

Students participate in numerous searches on the Internet. The project requires approximately two 60-minute sessions.

Q6. What intelligences can be brought into this Internet activity to help students gain understanding?

- *Verbal and Linguistic:* Students access text information through search results.
- *Intrapersonal:* Students evaluate search engines for personal needs.
- *Visual and Spatial:* Students assess home pages for spatial features and visual appearances.

Discovering Internet-Based Resources

The following search engines were selected for this activity because of their popularity with the general public and their practicality for students in their research. These search engines also show the variety of search engines available to users.

- Google (www.google.com)
- Google Scholar (www.googlescholar.com)
- Yahoo! Kids (http://kids.yahoo.com/)
- DMOZ (www.dmoz.org)
- AltaVista (www.altavista.com)
- Ask for Kids (www.askforkids.com)
- Dogpile (www.dogpile.com)
- HotBot (www.hotbot.com)

Stepping Out

Teachers use the following steps to guide the lesson process:

1. Introduce the activity to students. Discuss search engines and search techniques. Share Internet search techniques (Figure 4.3) with students. Explain that not all search engines are created equal; search engines can be rather different in the type of Web sites they return for the same exact search term. Therefore, it is important that students become aware of different search engines and learn some of their differences and unique qualities.
2. Pair students. Ask student pairs to choose a search term(s) that they will use to compare and contrast different search engines.
3. Give students time to use multiple search engines for the same search term. Ask students to compare and contrast the different search engines and evaluate them for usefulness. Tell students to write down their terms, what search engine they used, the number of Web sites returned for the search terms, and what observations they noticed about each search engine. (See Figure 4.4 for an information format that helps students display the information needed to compare and contrast the search engines.) Encourage students to spend time on each search engine's home page to learn about the options each one gives to help make the search more effective. For example, some search engines ask if the user wants only recent postings and others allow the user to specify what language the search engine should look for in selecting Web sites.

FAVORITES AND WEB SITE NOTEBOOKS

When exploring search engines, students and teachers quickly find sites they want to revisit at a later time. Teachers can take this opportunity to discuss using bookmarks or favorites and how they work. A great idea is to teach students to create an Internet notebook in which they list favorite Web sites and search engines and record comments and observations regarding different sites. If the class shares lab computers, students will most likely not be allowed to bookmark their favorite pages. However, teachers should show students how to use this feature. Most browsers simply use "Favorites" on the top menu bar; users can click there once they find a Web page they want to save. The Favorites drop-down menu then prompts the user to save the URL for the site, allowing the user to organize the pages in folders. This is a handy tool for revisiting sites.

ELECTRONIC MAIL

Electronic mail, or e-mail as it is affectionately called by millions of people, is used for anything that paper, mail, faxes, special delivery of documents, or

Search Engine Comparison Information

Search Engine: ______________________________

Two unique features of the home page:

1.

2.

Number of returned Web sites (hits): ____________________

____

Observation/comments about types of Web sites found: __________

____

____

Ranking: ______________________________

Figure 4.4

a telephone call does. E-mail continues to grow in popularity—thousands of people are beginning to use electronic messaging every day. E-mail is a networking vehicle. Despite the many tools available for accessing information over the Internet, e-mail remains the most useful application for many people. This is probably because e-mail is not merely about information—it is about human communication.

Teachers may choose one e-mail address for all students, especially in classrooms with only one computer. Another option is for teachers to supply each student with his or her own e-mail address. To familiarize students with using e-mail, teachers can ask students to send e-mail messages to classmates or to the teacher.

E-mail Smileys

Because e-mail is about human contact, it activates the interpersonal and intrapersonal intelligences as well as the verbal and linguistic intelligence. One way people make e-mail more personal is to use smileys (also called emoticons) to express emotions. Students enjoy learning about these small but important features they can add to their e-mail correspondence. Figure 4.5 shows a few common smileys.

E-mail Domains

Another helpful thing for students to learn is how to read an e-mail address to gain information about the sender. By looking at the final two or three letters in the e-mail address, students can recognize the domain from which the e-mail is sent. Domain designators represent either a type of organization, such as an educational institution, or a country, such as France. Figure 4.6 shows a few of the major e-mail address domains.

For example, for the e-mail address aperson@someorg.org, a student can quickly discern that the individual is using an address from a noncommercial organization. Domain names also exist for different countries, and in the United States each state has a domain name. For example, the e-mail address

Smileys

:)	Happiness	:-O	Shock
: (	Sadness	:-&	Tongue-tied
; -)	"Just kidding"	:'(	Crying
;->	Mischievousness	{}	Hugs
:-o	Surprise		

Figure 4.5

Domains

Domain Designator	Organization Type or Country
.edu	Educational institution
.com	Commercial organization
.net	Internet resource or access provider
.org	Noncommercial organization
.gov	Government office
.mil	Military site
.ca	Canada
.fr	France
.jp	Japan
.uk	United Kingdom
.us	United States

Figure 4.6

aperson@aschool.k12.ca.us shows that the e-mail address is located in California (ca), since it is followed by the United States (us) domain name. Without the United States domain designator, the "ca" would represent Canada instead of California. When "k12" appears in an e-mail address, the address is a school district somewhere in the United States.

E-mail Etiquette

Before students begin effective interpersonal correspondence projects, they need a general awareness and direct instruction in the skills of e-mail communication. Students use their interpersonal, intrapersonal, and verbal and linguistic intelligences while sending e-mail. As students correspond via e-mail, they need to keep in mind the following e-mail etiquette suggestions:

1. E-mail is fundamentally different from writing a letter or a note to someone because the turnaround time can be very fast. E-mail is more conversational.

2. E-mail messages do not include visual or auditory cues such as dress, diction, or dialect to help in the conversation. Therefore, the message receiver makes assumptions based on the sender's name, where the sender lives, and above all else, how the sender uses language to communicate.

3. E-mail messages do not convey emotions nearly as well as face-to-face or even telephone conversations because they lack vocal inflection,

gestures, and a shared environment. Therefore, students must learn to use language and expression to show emotion. For example, students may use ALL CAPS to express a strong emotion about a particular topic. They would not use ALL CAPS throughout the e-mail, because using ALL CAPS is the equivalent of shouting at the other person. Students should also be taught and reminded to use expressive descriptive words in their e-mail messages.

4. Students should use the subject line to give recipients an idea of the e-mail message's content.

INTERPERSONAL EXCHANGE ACTIVITIES

After students master the foundational skills of searching the Internet effectively and are generally aware of how to work with information after they find it, teachers can design lessons using the Internet and students' multiple intelligences. Interpersonal exchange activities are one of the most exciting ways to use the Internet within the curriculum. Simply said, these activities put students in touch with others outside of their familiar four classroom walls.

Interpersonal exchange activities use the personal intelligences as a jumping off point. Students call upon their interpersonal intelligence as they communicate and actually get to know others from around the nation and even the world. Teachers and students can take the opportunity to discuss the interpersonal intelligence and ways that students need to use this intelligence to communicate with others. Students also use their intrapersonal intelligence skills through these activities because the activities require students to recognize their own learning needs so that they might work with an expert or mentor in an area of study. Students need to understand themselves and their interests, hobbies, and opinions before they can truly share themselves with others. The strength or weakness of a student's intrapersonal intelligence skills affects his or her interpersonal intelligence skills. Therefore, interpersonal exchange activities provide a powerful forum for students to gain a deeper awareness of their personal intelligences as they work to understand a concept or learn a skill.

Interpersonal exchange activities come in many shapes and sizes. Some are simple and others are complex. The advantage of these types of activities is that they can easily be integrated with learning and understanding goals and tied directly to curricular standards. Figure 4.7 shows interpersonal exchange activities and how they can be connected to curricular areas and multiple intelligences.

Keypals

Keypal activities put students in touch with other students from around the nation and world. Keypals are the equivalent of old-fashioned pen pals, but instead of writing letters to one another, students send e-mail correspondence.

If teachers can find good keypal matches—matching students by age and curriculum similarities—keypals can be a wonderful way to reinforce and extend curricular learning. A keypal activity is one of the simplest and easiest ways for teachers to get their feet wet in Internet activities. The following "Taking It to the Classroom" activity uses keypals as an opportunity to teach students about reflective writing.

Types of Interpersonal Exchanges		
Interpersonal Exchange Activity	**Applicable Curricular Areas**	**Applicable Multiple Intelligences**
Keypals: Students in different geographic locations are paired together and communicate with one another via e-mail—the equivalent of pen pals.	language arts social studies	verbal/linguistic interpersonal intrapersonal
Telementoring: Subject matter specialists from all professions serve as electronic mentors for ongoing exploration of specific topics. Students can serve as telementors to other students.	social studies math science	verbal/linguistic interpersonal intrapersonal logical/mathematical naturalist
Global Classrooms: Two or more groups of students located anywhere in the world study a common topic, share what they learn, and produce a final product.	all	verbal/linguistic interpersonal logical/mathematical visual/spatial musical/rhythmic naturalist
Impersonations: Participants communicate with one another "in character."	social studies language arts visual and performing arts	verbal/linguistic interpersona/ visual/spatial
Questions and Answers: Students visit "ask-an-expert" sites, e-mail subject-specific questions to an expert in the field, and receive answers.	science math music	logical/mathematical verbal/linguistic intrapersonal naturalist musical/rhythmic
Electronic Appearances: Special guests can act as hosts via e-mail, chat rooms, newsgroups, and electronic bulletin boards so that students may communicate with them.	social studies language arts	verbal/linguistic interpersonal

Figure 4.7

Source: Adapted and reprinted with permission from Judi Harris, *Virtual Architecture: Designing and Directing Curriculum-Based Telecomputing*,

Taking It to the Classroom

Reflective Writing

The following activity uses an integrated curriculum approach to provide students with an opportunity to strengthen their reflective writing skills through a keypal activity. This lesson helps students understand the difference between reflective and other types of writing. Students gain a deep understanding of the process of reflection, what reflection is, how and why people reflect, and how reflection can be expressed in writing. Using a keypal activity is a natural fit. It teaches students what e-mail is, how to use it, and what etiquette is expected from e-mail users. Keypal activities are an easy way for students to begin learning just how interactive the Internet can be. This activity is appropriate for students in grades 4 to 12.

Brain-Compatibility Link

Focus Links: Relevance and Meaning, Making Connections

One of the main pursuits of the human brain is to seek connections, patterns, and chunks of information that fit together (Caine & Caine, 1991). To assist the brain in this pursuit, learning should include authentic and practical problems, projects, and dilemmas that increase *relevance* and *meaning* for students. This reflective writing activity strives to strengthen students' writing skills by providing a meaningful and challenging way to do so. By asking students to write reflectively to their keypals, teachers prompt students to use several of their intelligences as they make a *connection* between a style of writing and a current-day purpose for using such a writing style.

Charting the Way

The preplanning questions help guide the lesson to meet goals and objectives.

Q1. What are the deep understandings of this activity?

Students understand what reflective writing is and how it is different from other types of writing.

Q2. What skills and knowledge, both academic and Internet-based, will students strengthen as a result of this activity?

Students learn to conduct e-mail correspondence on a regular basis.
Students learn and practice e-mail etiquette.

Q3. What facts do students need to become familiar with through this activity?

Students learn that reflective writing can be used in e-mail and personal correspondences.

Students learn what e-mail is and how it is used in person-to-person correspondence.

Q4. How can students' understanding, knowledge, and skills be assessed?

The Understanding Rubric provides a valuable assessment tool for teachers and students in this activity. Students must keep the big picture in mind; it is more important that they understand reflective writing and reflection than it is that they hit it off with their keypals. Therefore, teachers can use the generalized Understanding Rubric (Figure 3.4 and in Appendix B) to assess how well students can explain and interpret reflective writing and apply this knowledge with a fresh perspective, empathy, and self-knowledge.

Students submit three examples of reflective writing shown in their e-mail correspondences with their keypals. Students select any three, but must highlight the sentences and paragraphs within the e-mail that show reflection.

Q5. What type of Internet activity will help students reach these learning goals? What will the Internet activity entail? How long will the activity last?

Web sites supporting keypal activity are used. The activity uses the Internet to connect students for their e-mail activity. Four to six 60-minute sessions are needed for this activity. Students need 20–25 minutes every day or so to check their e-mails and return messages.

Q6. What intelligences can be brought into this Internet activity to help students gain understanding?

- *Verbal and linguistic:* Students work on their writing skills.
- *Interpersonal:* Students stay in touch with a keypal throughout this activity.
- *Intrapersonal:* Students practice reflecting on their feelings and thoughts.

Discovering Internet-Based Resources

The following Web sites provide teachers with keypal opportunities for their students. Teachers simply visit the site to register their classes to participate. These Web sites were selected for their ease in registration and their ability to match classrooms from around the nation and the world.

- Epals (www.epals.com)
- Heinemann Interactive (www.hi.com.au)
- Intercultural E-Mail Classroom Connections (www.iecc.org)

(*Note:* These and additional sites are listed in Appendix A.)

Stepping Out

Teachers use the following steps to guide the lesson process:

1. Discuss the concept of reflection. Begin the reflective writing lesson by introducing students to the concept of reflection by having students look at small mirrors and discuss what they see. Using the analogy of the mirror, discuss reflection in daily life and ask students to identify times they would use reflection and why.
2. Share and discuss reflection in writing. After all students are familiar with reflection, turn the discussion to how reflection is used as a writing style. Give specific examples of writers and stories that display reflection. Ask students to compare and contrast reflective, narrative, and expository writing styles.
3. Introduce the concept of keypals and review e-mail etiquette. Tell students that they will exchange e-mail with a keypal. Ask them to reflect on what they want to know about their keypals and what they want to share about themselves. Finally, using one of the Internet services, match students with keypals.
4. Tell students that they should use reflective writing in their keypal exchanges. Give students the following guiding questions to help their reflective process as well as provide discussion points along the way:
   a. What do you want to learn about your keypal?
   b. What would you like to know about where your keypal lives?
   c. What is the hardest part about describing yourself to someone else?
   d. What was your reaction to your first message?
   e. What makes good e-mail messages and good e-mail writing?
5. After students have had several rounds of correspondence with their keypals, ask them to share the answers to the questions and discuss the process of reflective writing.
6. Complete the activity by asking students to submit examples of reflective writing from their keypal correspondences, to print messages they sent, and to highlight where they used reflection in their writing.

Telementoring

Telementoring places students in touch with adults and older students in a mentoring relationship. A wonderful example of an ongoing telementoring project is a sixth grade teacher in Massachusetts who matched his students with a mentor called a netpal. The mentor is notified via e-mail that his or her student has posted a writing assignment on a specified Web site. The mentor visits the site, reads about the assignment, reads the student's assignment, and provides feedback and constructive suggestions via e-mail to the student. This gives students a real-world contact and ongoing feedback about their writing skills. It increases their motivation to write and also to write well.

As the availability and reliability of networked communication systems grow, so does interest in using the Internet to facilitate lifelong learning experiences that connect people from different communities, professions, and generations. Telementoring promises a powerful way to make learning more relevant and personal for a wide range of students.

In the K–12 education environment, several telementoring models are being explored. These models range in duration from a few weeks to years and vary in mentoring format to include one-to-one, moderated group, unmoderated group, and peer mentoring. The purpose of the mentoring may be to provide information on specific subjects, such as western expansion or satellite exploration, or it may be to give insight and guidance on life goals and choices. Whatever the case, all telementoring models use e-mail or the Internet to facilitate communication among students, teachers, and professionals in the outside world. A great example of telementoring projects can be found at The College of William & Mary's Electronic Emissary Project at emissary.wm.edu. In addition, there are many sites that help connect mentors and students, such as the Telementoring Web site at www.telementoring.org.

What makes a telementoring relationship work? Research suggests that several factors contribute to its success.

1. Frequency of contact is paramount. Students and their mentors should try to communicate at least once a week. Protracted silences often lead to misunderstandings or disinterest. Realistic and explicit time and communication frequency estimates should be designated.
2. Preparation is recommended. Clearly conceived learning goals for the project should be articulated to both student and telementor. Teachers and telementors should communicate before the project begins. This helps mentors become more sensitive to how students might interpret written feedback and comments. Similarly, students should also be prepared for the experience. They can create short biographies of themselves and brainstorm questions for their mentors.
3. Mentor-student matching is not an exact science. However, research indicates that matches are most successful when students have some say in the selection of their mentors. When mentors share both personal and career information, they help build stronger relationships with their mentees. Students express greater satisfaction when mentors refer to the personal details students share and relate these details to their own experiences.

Lynn Takacs, a teacher in San Juan Capistrano, California, has created a wonderful example of a telementor project for a fifth grade social studies class. Takacs uses a step-by-step lesson design format. She begins her unit on explorers by dividing her class into five cooperative groups that are assigned to learn about, analyze, and design a Web site about a famous explorer. Takacs provides students with essential questions that help frame their research: What does it take to be an explorer? What is so special about this explorer? How did your explorer change the course of history? Are there current-day explorers who might be changing the course of history?

Takacs then links each group with a telementor they can communicate with via e-mail for assistance throughout the project. Takacs gives each telementor information about the explorer unit, the cooperative group they are working with, and what the final product will be. Each group then goes about researching and writing up their information, organizing it in a coherent way, and designing a Web site for that explorer. The groups contact their telementor via e-mail to read the group's latest writing, to critique and offer feedback on it, to assist in finding information about the explorer, and to provide feedback on the Web site they create.

This telementoring project is powerful. It is designed around deep understanding questions, provides students with opportunities to use their different intelligences, and allows students to reap the benefits of a telementor relationship. Takacs' steps for creating a successful telementor project are recapped in Figure 4.8.

By providing students with telementors, teachers can increase enthusiasm for an activity, because students quickly become aware that their work will be shared outside of the classroom's walls. Immediate feedback from and communication with a telementor provides students with the motivation to continually improve the quality of their work.

Global Classrooms

In global classrooms, two or more classrooms study a common topic together. Global classroom projects work well in classrooms that have telecommuting capabilities and succeed when focused by topic and by curriculum. In a good global classroom project, objectives and outcomes are clearly defined, and each participant agrees with the objectives and outcomes. The best global projects promote collaboration through a Web page or consistent e-mail correspondence. Global projects usually occur over a period of days, weeks, or even years. They vary in the degree of commitment required of teachers and students. Some projects address only one subject matter, while others integrate many disciplines.

Steps to a Successful Telementoring Project

1. Form student groups.
2. Recruit telementors and provide information about the project and students.
3. Give students the big picture of what they are learning, using questions as guides.
4. Pair student groups and telementors.
5. Students research and work with activity.
6. Students share work with telementor for ongoing feedback and help.
7. Final product is shared with telementor.

Figure 4.8

Many project registry sites are available on the Internet. Some registries allow teachers to post their project ideas and find other classrooms and teachers interested in participating. (Some teachers find it easier to start as participants in a project, rather than design their own projects.) Other registries feature projects designed by businesses, universities, organizations, and grant recipients. For example, NASA and the Annenburg Foundation have developed a number of online projects that are appropriate for students in Grades 4 to 12. These sites promote classrooms working together to study a common theme or curricular area and to produce a single product.

One outstanding example of a global classroom project is Learning Circles on iEARN (www.iearn.org/circles). This site provides teachers with easy access to joining a project that fits their curriculum. An example learning circle activity is the Computer Chronicles. The activity's theme is promoting writing across the curriculum, and it revolves around producing a newspaper called *The Computer Chronicles.* Each class sponsors one or more sections of the newspaper as its learning circle project. They solicit articles from their partner classes and edit them to create a section of the newspaper. This section is combined with the other sections sponsored by circles partners to form the completed newspaper.

Questions and Answers

The Internet includes many sites where students can pose questions to knowledgeable adults and receive answers in a timely manner. Most of these sites are "ask-an-expert" sites where students can visit as frequently as needed. They may ask a geologist about rock formation, an astronomer about a potentially new planet, or a mathematician about a difficult calculus equation. Examples of these sites include:

- Ask An Expert (www.askanexpert.com)
- Ask Dr. Universe (www.wsu.edu/DrUniverse)
- Ask a Scientist (www.madsci.org/submit.html)
- Ask Wendell (yucky.discovery.com/flash/askwendell/index.html)

Teachers use question-and-answer sites to promote guided inquiry with students. Teachers pose a question to raise students' curiosity and allow them to find answers to meaningful and essential questions.

For example, a teacher who is teaching about hurricanes might pose the question, Why is the eye of a storm so calm? Or, is there really such a thing as a calm before the storm and why would it happen? As students form their own questions to ask an online expert, the teacher provides good examples of questions to ask. When students formulate simplistic questions to ask the expert, the teacher must show students how to ask more complex, rich, and deep questions.

Teachers must ask themselves when question-and-answer Internet activities are most useful and what purpose these activities should serve. Teachers can use these activities when they want to demonstrate how to find answers to puzzling questions. Question-and-answer activities are especially pertinent when the teacher cannot sufficiently answer a student's question. Teachers can say to students, "Let's figure this out together." Students and teachers then turn to experts in the field for answers. By doing so, the teacher models what lifelong learning is all about and promotes students' intellectual curiosity.

In addition, question-and-answer activities can strengthen and stimulate students' multiple intelligences by putting students in touch with an expert in specific intelligence areas. For example, students could ask musicians to discuss their rise to prominence (musical and rhythmic intelligence) or ask botanists to share a complex plant classification system (naturalist intelligence). One of the greatest benefits of using the Internet in the classroom is providing students with the opportunity to learn about topics and subjects that the classroom teacher may not know all that much about.

Impersonations

In impersonation activities, one or all of the participants communicate with each other in character. Individual students and full classes can impersonate historical or famous individuals as two or more classrooms study similar subjects. A history professor at a university may impersonate James Madison and communicate via e-mail with elementary students who are studying American history.

Impersonations can be the electronic equivalent of classroom role playing. Traditionally, a teacher asks a student or group of students to pretend to be a famous historical character and to act out a short skit for the class. In an electronic impersonation, a student or group of students pretends to be a famous person, goes online, and impersonates that character for other classes. Impersonation can be done via classroom Web sites. Other classrooms visit the site on a regular basis to learn more about a famous person's life, and they also receive e-mail from that famous person. For creative teachers, impersonations offer a wonderful way of teaching students about specific people while making the experience alive and meaningful.

Electronic Appearances

Electronic appearances feature guests with whom students can correspond via e-mail, chat rooms, newsgroups, and bulletin boards. Some Web sites host electronic appearances by individuals who offer students and classrooms information and added experience in a certain curriculum area.

For example, the educational Web site, Scholastic (www.teacher.scholastic.com), hosts author forums. During a forum, an author goes online to answer questions and provide information about the writing and reading process. Another good example is the Women of NASA site (www.quest.arc.nasa.gov/women/intro.html). This site profiles female scientists and hosts live chats during which students can communicate with women about their careers and training.

Many teachers use electronic appearances to motivate their students. These appearances are the Internet version of asking a local community member to come into the classroom to talk to students.

Both impersonations and electronic appearances allow students a wonderful opportunity to use their interpersonal intelligence skills as they gain a personal perspective of a career or a specific person. It is one thing for students to discuss the life of a famous author and quite another for students to communicate personally with that author. For students who are strong in the personal intelligences, these activities make a significant difference in their engagement, motivation, and retention of information.

5

Enhancing Information-Gathering and Analysis Skills

The amount of information on the Internet is staggering by any account. As more and more classrooms use the Internet, the amount of information filtering into K–12 classrooms around the world is mind-boggling. This information explosion has created a wonderful challenge for many and a frustrating dilemma for others.

When the Internet began to make its way into classrooms, many educators sounded the trumpets and heralded the end of education as it had been known. It was a brave new world—knowledge was being delivered through a vehicle other than a teacher! The sage on the stage days were over! Yet as time went on, it became clear that there was a huge difference between information and knowledge. Many researchers and writers in the field of educational technology believe that confusing knowledge and information is perhaps one of the most serious mistakes in the use of information technology. The confusion leads to the attitude that giving students information is the same as giving them knowledge.

As most, if not all, teachers know, knowledge and information are hugely different. *Information* is delivered like a package to a doorstep. It arrives in an enormous quantity and in variations as words on a screen, pictures, video clips, and sound bites. Knowledge is not so easily delivered or recognized. *Knowledge* is the result of receiving information, actively working with it, and personally transforming it so that it makes sense and is useful. Teachers must recognize this critical difference between information and knowledge because the difference significantly influences the creation and use of Internet-based learning activities. The most motivating activities ask students to collect and share information, and then use it to produce or create a product or idea. Within this process, students can transform information into knowledge.

Teachers can help students with this vital process by introducing them to information literacy skills. Before students participate in information-gathering and analysis activities—collecting, compiling, and comparing different types of information—teachers must introduce students to information literacy skills that help them transform the incredible quantity of information into usable knowledge and deep understanding.

INFORMATION LITERACY SKILLS

For many teachers, their memories of completing a research report focus on being assigned a topic, being sent to the library, feeling lucky if they could find more than one resource (with the encyclopedia serving as the main source), and writing up the report using their own words. Most frequently, their biggest problem was not being able to find enough information from outdated books and encyclopedias.

Fast-forward to the twenty-first century. The amount of information available over the Internet, on the news, and in newspapers, magazines, and books is astonishing—and overwhelming. Students now are literally surrounded with Web pages of information, CD-ROMs with interactive programs, books, magazines, and other multimedia products. Most frequently, the biggest problem students face is finding too much information and not knowing what to do with it. Before students can be taught to understand concepts and skills and be asked to use their multiple intelligences, they need specific tools to work with the large amount of information at their fingertips. Without these skills, students feel like innocent lambs being thrown to the information wolves.

Disturbing trends about finding information and doing research are developing in students. The top three are (1) students believing that anything from a computer is better than anything that comes from a book, (2) students viewing the library as a last resort, and (3) students being concerned more with the quantity than with the quality of their sources. It is critical that students learn to find information from many sources and be able to analyze its quality relatively quickly. Only then are they able to move to the next step of using the information to produce a piece of work. These searching and analyzing skills are information literacy skills, and the sooner teachers begin helping students learn them, the better the students' chances are of succeeding in the Information Age.

In a time when many are crying for back-to-basics in schools throughout the United States, teachers need to carefully evaluate what the basics are for students living in the twenty-first century. Reading, writing, and arithmetic are still at the top of the list, but basic skills also include being able to find, analyze, and work with information. Teachers can no longer expect to fill their students' heads with content and assume the students are prepared for the future. Information literacy skills now join reading, writing, and arithmetic as basic skills of the twenty-first century.

Michael Eisenberg and Doug Johnson (1996) propose six components of information literacy skills in their Big6 skills approach (www.big6.com). Figure 5.1 briefly lists the information literacy skills with the Bloom taxonomy skill that it relates to in parentheses. Teachers may want to post this list in their classrooms because these skills need to be seen and discussed on a regular basis.

Know When There Is a Need for Information (Comprehension)

Knowing that information is needed means students

1. recognize when there is a need for information to solve a problem or develop an idea;
2. brainstorm multiple strategies for approaching the identified problem or issue; and
3. identify, organize, and sequence tasks to complete an information-based project.

First, students need to identify the problem they are trying to solve and the exact information they are trying to learn. This is a critical step because students must have their end goal in mind. Second, students write down the steps needed to complete their research or to find an answer. Many students use their logical and mathematical intelligence as they learn to create sequential plans. Students may conduct their own searches, find an online expert, or do an online simulation to gather information.

Classroom technological activities to help students practice this information literacy skill include asking students to

1. use e-mail and online discussion groups on the Internet to communicate with teachers regarding assignments, tasks, and information problems;
2. use desktop conferencing and e-mail to generate topics and problems and to facilitate cooperative activities among local student groups; and
3. use computer brainstorming or idea-generating software to define or refine the information problem, including developing a research question or perspective on a topic. (Many brainstorming software programs ask students to use their visual and spatial intelligence to organize information. This assists students who naturally organize information with this intelligence, yet struggle when asked to use a logical and mathematical or verbal and linguistic approach.)

Information Literacy Skills

1. Know when there is a need for information. (Comprehension)
2. Find and identify the information needed. (Comprehension and Analysis)
3. Analyze the information. (Analysis and Evaluation)
4. Organize the information. (Application)
5. Use the information effectively to address the problem or task. (Synthesis)
6. Communicate the information and evaluate the results. (Application and Evaluation)

Figure 5.1

Note: Adapted from "Computer Skills for Information Problem Solving: Learning and Teaching Technology in Context" by M. B. Eisenberg and D. Johnson. *ERIC Digest:* March, 1996. (ED392463)

Find and Identify the Information Needed (Comprehension and Analysis)

Finding and identifying information needed helps students to

1. formulate questions based on information needs,
2. use effective search techniques and keywords to search for information,
3. analyze various sources for relevance, and
4. read competently so that they understand the information presented.

Students need to learn to formulate well-defined questions that relate to their identified needs, problems, or research. Teachers should remind students to search for information using their multiple intelligences. Students may search for information about their problem or issue that relates to specific intelligences. For example, students searching for information about Greece can look for information about Greek art, sports, music, and family life instead of simply reading books and searching Internet sites for general information. By doing this, students explore and awaken their intelligences throughout the research process. Figure 5.2 offers questions to prompt students in their information gathering.

Students can also be encouraged to gain multiple perspectives on a subject, especially a controversial one. Teachers can challenge students to search for opposing viewpoints or to look for opinions or thoughts from different people involved in the same period of history or the same event.

Teachers should allow students to practice their searching skills or direct students to specific Web sites where their questions can be answered. Teachers may either preview all sites or develop and express a degree of comfort with students' searching skills and responsibility levels and allow students to search on their own. In both instances, students determine what suggested resources are most likely to meet their needs.

Classroom technological activities to help students practice this information literacy skill include asking students to

1. assess the value of various types of electronic resources for data gathering, including databases, CD-ROM resources, commercial and Internet online resources, electronic reference works, and community and government information electronic resources;
2. identify and apply specific criteria for evaluating computerized electronic resources;
3. assess the value of e-mail and online discussion groups on the Internet as part of a search of the current literature or in relation to the information task;
4. use computers to generate modifiable flowcharts, charts, time lines, organizational charts, project plans, and calendars that help students plan and organize complex or group information problem-solving tasks; and
5. effectively use search techniques to gather information from the Internet.

Analyze the Information (Analysis and Evaluation)

To show the skill of analysis, students need to be able to

1. evaluate the quality of information by establishing authority;
2. determine accuracy and authenticity; and
3. distinguish between opinion, reasoned arguments, and fact.

These skills are very complex and can take a lifetime to learn. Teachers can begin discussing these strategies with students at any age. One powerful way of teaching students is to show examples of what an opinion looks like versus what a reasoned argument or fact looks like. Teachers can find Web site examples of each and show students that not everything on the Internet is factual.

It is critical that students do not equate a textbook with the Internet. Many students believe that if they read it in a book or see it on the Internet, it has to be true. Many believe that to be published on the Internet, authors must prove their information is accurate. It is important for students to understand that anyone can publish a Web page and that Web pages are not vetted for accuracy or truth—they may contain false or inaccurate information. Therefore, students need to learn to eye all information with a healthy cynicism, while they search and find supporting information. Students should look for information about the author or sponsoring organization to establish authority and authenticity. Students can also look for multiple sources regarding the same topic as a way of determining the accuracy and authenticity of the information.

Multiple Intelligences Information-Gathering Suggestions

Verbal/Linguistic

What do books and magazines tell me about the topic? Is there information I can get from the computer and Internet? Have I tried the school library and the public library? Do my parents have any books at home that can help?

Logical/Mathematical

What information can I find about the economy or costs of the topic? Is there any financial information I can find? Can I use technology tools to gather data?

Visual/Spatial

Are there photographs I can use in my report? Can I draw a map or picture about what I have learned? Are there charts or graphics that can give me valuable information? Is there any other way I can illustrate the important parts of my report?

Musical/Rhythmic

Is there any music that teaches me about the topic? Are there any songs or musical history events that relate to the topic? Are there videos that can provide me with information?

Bodily/Kinesthetic

Are there dances that relate to the topic? Are there plays or skits written about the topic that will give me information? Are any sports related to the topic?

Interpersonal

What do people around me know about the topic—my parents, grandparents, sisters, brothers, aunts, uncles, friends? Do I trust that their information is correct? Do I know how they learned this information?

Intrapersonal

What do I already know about the topic? How do I know this information is correct? Where did I learn this information? Do I already have strong opinions and feelings about this topic?

Naturalist

Do nature and wildlife relate to my topic? If so, why are they important? Do plants and animals have a role in my topic?

Figure 5.2

Classroom technological activities to help students practice this information literacy skill include asking students to

1. locate and use appropriate computer resources and technologies available within the school library media center, including those on the local area network (e.g., online catalogs, periodical indexes, full-text sources, multimedia computer stations, CD-ROM stations, online terminals, scanners, and digital cameras);
2. locate and use appropriate computer resources and technologies available beyond the school through the Internet;
3. know the roles and computer expertise of the people working in the school library media center and elsewhere who might provide information or assistance;
4. use electronic reference materials available through the Internet;
5. use the Internet to reach experts, help, and referral services; and
6. conduct self-initiated electronic surveys through e-mail, Listserv, or newsgroups.

Organize the Information (Application)

The information literacy skill of organizing information helps students to

1. know how knowledge is organized;
2. organize and store data in searchable formats; and
3. organize information for practical application.

After students access and analyze information, they must learn to organize it so it can be found easily for future reference and use. Students need to know how to bookmark pages and use folders within the bookmark section. Students may wish to print out specific pages and use graphic organizers or outlines to organize information. They may organize their information using an overall task list or questions as guiding topics. To help students organize information, teachers must remind them to practice the first two information literacy skills.

Not all students remember or organize information in the same way. The process of organizing information physically and mentally relates to a person's most frequently used intelligences. Some students use their personal intelligences to discuss and organize their information while working with a peer or adult. Other students use their verbal and linguistic intelligence and literally think out loud to organize information into a clear structure and format. Still others use their visual and spatial intelligence to create mind maps and idea webs to organize their information. Those strong in the logical and mathematical intelligence may use a sequential outline or a chronological list. This variety can be difficult for teachers who habitually organize information in a format that works best for them. Yet by providing students with options to choose an organization scheme for themselves, teachers employ brain-compatible teaching strategies that result in better student understanding and retention of information.

Classroom technological activities to help students practice this information literacy skill include asking students to

1. view, download, and open documents and programs from Internet sites;
2. cut and paste information from an electronic source into a personal document using proper citation;
3. use bookmarks and folders to organize Web sites;
4. take notes and outline with a word processor or similar program;
5. record electronic sources of information and locations of those sources to properly cite and credit them in footnotes, endnotes, and bibliographies;
6. use electronic spreadsheets, databases, and statistical software to process and analyze statistical data; and
7. analyze and filter electronic information in relation to the task, while rejecting nonrelevant information.

Use the Information Effectively to Address the Problem or Task (Synthesis)

Students are using information effectively when they

1. create new information by synthesizing data from primary and secondary sources,
2. integrate new information to existing knowledge, and
3. summarize information found in sources.

After students analyze and organize information, they must learn to put it all together. Using their newly found information and knowledge, students summarize what they have learned as it relates to the identified tasks and questions. It is important for students to recognize their own existing knowledge about the subject. Students should learn to ask themselves if the new information fits with what they already know or if it is different. In addition, students must learn to differentiate between primary and secondary sources and to recognize that the Internet offers only secondary source information.

Classroom technological activities to help students practice this information literacy skill include asking students to

1. classify and group information using a word processor, database, or spreadsheet;
2. use word processing and desktop publishing software to create printed documents;
3. develop keyboard skills equivalent to at least twice the rate of handwriting speed;
4. create and use computer-generated graphics in various print and electronic presentations;

5. use software to create original spreadsheets and databases;
6. generate charts, tables, and graphs using electronic spreadsheets and other graphing programs;
7. use e-mail and other telecommunications capabilities to share information and products;
8. use specialized computer applications as appropriate for specific tasks (e.g., music composition software, computer-assisted drawing programs, and mathematics software); and
9. properly cite and credit electronic sources in footnotes, endnotes, and bibliographies.

Communicate the Information and Evaluate the Results (Application and Evaluation)

The information literacy skill of communication and evaluation supports students as they

1. present information in a final product form,
2. document sources using appropriate formats, and
3. perform ongoing evaluation by revising and updating the product.

Students now turn their attention to producing an end product with their information and knowledge. Teachers should show students examples of well-done final products; these may be reports, drawings, oral presentations, or multimedia products.

In addition, teachers can have students create Web pages as final products. Some teachers choose to have different student groups create their own Web pages and then combine them all to make a Web site that culminates in a classroom unit. But this may be too time-consuming for some lessons. If a group of students spend weeks of their learning time creating an elaborate Web site that will not be viewed by others for any length of time, it may be wiser for the teacher to pass on the Web site and use classroom time for other learning activities. Teachers may compromise by creating a yearlong summary Web site for a class or group of students. With this choice, students practice Web site design and use time to summarize what they have learned throughout the year.

Whatever end product teachers use, they should share with students how they will be assessed before explaining the end product requirements or the learning activity itself. Teachers may share rubrics and clearly outline how students' work will be assessed. For example, teachers can share with students the Information Literacy Skills Rubric discussed in Chapter 3 (and shown in Appendix B). This rubric can be applied to a myriad of different activities and be used to constantly remind students about these important skills.

Classroom technological activities to help students practice this information literacy skill include asking students to

1. evaluate electronic presentations in terms of both the content and format;
2. use spell-checking and grammar-checking capabilities of word processing and other software to edit and revise their work;
3. understand and abide by online etiquette when sending e-mail, reading newsgroups, and visiting two-way communication sites such as bulletin boards, message boards, and social sites;
4. reflect thoughtfully on the use of electronic resources and tools throughout the process;
5. use presentation software (e.g., PowerPoint) to create electronic slide shows and to generate overheads and slides;
6. create hypermedia and multimedia productions with digital video and audio; and
7. create Web pages.

One of the final steps in any product is to document where the information was found. Using a bibliography format, students should record Web site addresses, the name of the sites, and other important information such as the authors of the sites. In general, the teacher must tell students what information they need to identify so that the information is clear to a reader. The following examples show a general format for referencing Web sites and e-mail addresses, although there are many acceptable ways to cite electronic messages.

- Web page references should display the author's name if available, the title of the Web site in italics, the date the Web site was posted or last updated, the URL in brackets, and the date the site was accessed. For example,

  Eisenberg, Mike and Berkowitz, Bob, *The Big6.* [http://www.big6.com], 2001–2005 Big6 Associates, LLC.

If the source is a magazine or newspaper article found on the Internet, the citation would look like this:

  Smith, Mary. "The Long Days of War." (6/3/05). [http://www.LATimes.org]. *Historical Society Annual Publications.* 8/15/00.

- E-mail references can include the writer's name, subject line in quotation marks, the e-mail address, and date of message. For example,

  Jones, Jerry. "Civil War was a . . ." [JJones@aol.com], 8/10/04.

Information literacy skills entail complex thinking and reasoning. These skills take time and practice to learn. Teachers can teach the information literacy skills to students in the following ways:

1. Introduce the information literacy skills to students. Teachers should explain the skills and why they are important. This introduction helps develop a common language that can be shared by students and teachers

for the remainder of the year. Teachers can introduce or review the Information Literacy Skills Rubric shown in Figure 3.6 and Appendix B.

2. Model the use of information literacy skills by thinking out loud. This process consists of the teacher thinking out loud when he or she is identifying a problem, finding information, analyzing information, using information, and producing a piece of work. Teachers can also ask students to model their thought processes through the different stages of working with information. As students watch teachers and other students manage information, think out loud about what is being analyzed, and reach conclusions, they begin to use similar strategies themselves. In addition, their intrapersonal intelligence can be strengthened as they use metacognition and analysis to learn these skills.
3. Give students ongoing opportunities to review and practice the skills within the context of a topic of study.
4. Carefully supervise and give feedback to students in their first attempts at using these skills. This helps students develop correct habits from the beginning.
5. Provide repeated opportunities to practice and receive individual feedback. Students can be asked to provide feedback to a peer and to help others develop their information literacy skills. In doing so, the student not only strengthens his or her skills but also uses interpersonal intelligence.
6. Begin with simple practice exercises and gradually move into more complex instruction and practice.

As teachers work through the information literacy skills with students, they must remember that this requires very complex thinking and organizing. Therefore, students need multiple lessons and practice sessions. Students are always on a continuum of improvement with these skills—this is not a situation where students either do or do not have the skill. Teachers also need to continually strengthen these valuable skills. The following classroom activity provides an example of how teachers can integrate the information literacy skills into their lessons.

Taking It to the Classroom

Mini–Research Project

After all six information literacy skills have been introduced, discussed, and practiced, teachers can use the following activity to help students in Grades 4 to 12 work with each skill in a conscious way. As the skills become more familiar and common to students, teachers can embed them in research and Internet-based activities. This activity provides an opportunity for students to work with these skills in a mini–research project.

Brain-Compatibility Link

Focus Links: Choice, Meaning and Relevance, Prior Knowledge

In this mini–research activity, the teacher asks students to select an issue or problem to study and learn about and to choose a final product to complete. Providing students with *choice* is a brain-compatible strategy that engages students in their learning. When students select their own topics, they are inherently more interested in and motivated by the activity. The ability to choose their topics also increases the level of *meaning* and *relevance*. Students are also asked to write what they already know about their topic or problem before beginning their research. By doing this, they access their *prior knowledge* about the topic and are well on their way to learning more.

Charting the Way

The preplanning questions help guide the lesson to meet goals and objectives.

Q1. What are the deep understandings of this activity?

Students gain a deeper understanding of the information literacy skills and recognize that the skills work together to assist in their research project efforts.

Q2. What skills and knowledge, both academic and Internet-based, will students strengthen as a result of this activity?

Students strengthen their basic searching skills on the Internet.

Students strengthen their skills in searching for information through the lens of multiple intelligences using the information-gathering strategies.

Students strengthen their research skills, especially their ability to find and organize information via the Internet.

Q3. What facts do students need to become familiar with through this activity?

Students become more familiar with different search engines.

Students are introduced to different ways to organize information via their study groups.

Q4. How can students' understanding, knowledge, and skills be assessed?

Students complete a final product showing their research process and using the information literacy skills. Students select one of three products: a summary, a Web site, or an oral presentation.

The Information Literacy Skills Rubric (Figure 3.6 and in Appendix B) is shared with students and used as an evaluation at the end of the project.

Q5. What type of Internet activity will help students reach these learning goals? What will the Internet project entail? How long will the activity last?

The project may take up to two weeks and is a research-oriented activity. Students use the Internet as an informational resource and get practice working on the Internet, using search engines, and practicing using their information literacy skills.

Q6. What intelligences can be brought into this Internet activity to help students gain understanding?

- *Verbal and linguistic:* Students participate in research.
- *Visual and spatial:* Students create a Web page using this intelligence.
- *Interpersonal:* Students work in study groups to share their research.
- *Intrapersonal:* Students choose to work on a project of interest. Teachers can also encourage students to use their multiple intelligences through the information-gathering process.

Discovering Internet-Based Resources

The following Web sites provide further information and additional links that relate to the information literacy skills. These Web sites were chosen because they thoroughly explain these skills and provide in-depth information about each one.

- Mankato Schools Information Literacy Curriculum Guidelines (www.isd77.k12.mn.us/resources/infocurr/infolit.html)
- Essential Skills for Information Literacy (www.wlma.org/informationliteracy)
- School-Libraries.Org (www.school-libraries.org/resources/literacy.html)

Stepping Out

Teachers use the following steps to guide the lesson process.

1. Review the information literacy skills.
2. Brainstorm issues and problems and ask students to select a topic to study. Students may need help generating a list of these types of problems or issues from which to choose.
3. Share the Information Literacy Skills Rubric (Figure 3.6 and in Appendix B) with students.

4. Explain that the purpose of this activity is to help students practice their information literacy skills. They use these skills as they use the Internet and other resources to gather information and research topics. Tell students that they may meet with you at different times to discuss their topics and research plans. In addition, students may be assigned to a study group that meets periodically to share research progress and final products.

5. Give students class time to research and collect information. Remember to discuss ways students will need to collect and record their information. Consider guiding their research process by asking or discussing with them the following issues:
   a. What topic would you like to research or what problem would you like to examine in greater detail for a solution? What information do you need to collect based on your identified research topic or problem?
   b. Formulate five questions that need to be answered based on the information you need to find. Brainstorm five sources where you can look for information. Use the Multiple Intelligences Information-Gathering Suggestions (Figure 5.2). Use your Internet searching skills to assist your information searches.
   c. After you have found some information from identified sources, explain why you think the information you found is accurate and true. Comment on whether the information includes facts, opinions, or a reasoned argument. After you have collected your information, organize it based on what you feel is the most relevant information you found. You can use mind maps, outlines, note cards, or any other way to organize the information as long as you can explain it to your study group. Remember to organize it in a way that makes sense to you and that you will be able to use in the future.

6. Give students three choices for a completed project.
   a. **Summary.** Write a three-to four-page summary of the problem or topic including what information was needed, sources, and what was learned about the topic. Make a special point to highlight how you used the Internet as well as how you used the multiple intelligences in collecting information or organizing it. Be sure to cite any resources used at the end of the summary.
   b. **Web Page.** Create a Web page design for others to visit that introduces the problem or research topic. The site should explain the topic and what information is linked to the topic, and it should include a summary of the problem or topic area. Remember to use visual representations. Cite any resources you used somewhere on the Web page.
   c. **Oral Presentation.** Create an oral presentation to be given to the class. Use PowerPoint or another electronic software system to create presentation visual displays. The presentation should explain the topic and what information is linked to the topic, and it should give a summary of the problem or topic area. Use visual graphics or pictures to illustrate the topic.

7. Ask students to share their summary, Web page, or oral presentation with their study group. Allow five to eight minutes for each student to share his or her work. Ask study groups to evaluate each member's project and discuss it with the creator. After all members of the study group have shared, ask the group to vote on one presentation to share with the class. The selected presentation should be a good example of the information literacy skills, describe an interesting topic, and include an excellent final product.

INFORMATION-GATHERING AND ANALYSIS ACTIVITIES

A number of information-gathering and analysis Internet activities are available to help students practice their information literacy skills (see Figure 5.3). These activities focus on providing students with experiences in gathering, organizing, and sharing data with others via the Internet. Many students are more motivated and enthusiastic about working with information when they know their work will be shared with a large audience. These activities support development of students' information literacy skills, because they provide a structure and meaning for students to gather, organize, analyze, and use information.

Information Exchanges

Information exchange activities continue to grow and expand on the Internet. In a nutshell, these activities involve classes around the world in collecting information about a topic, and then sharing information on a Web site for eventual synthesis and evaluation. Topics range from book reviews to weather conditions, school ecosystems to money conversions. Teachers can discover what types of information exchanges are available by spending time visiting Internet examples.

The Kidlink site (www.kidlink.org) offers excellent examples of information exchanges divided into curriculum areas, and helps teachers find sites of interest easily. This site also offers excellent examples of information exchanges that fit naturally into the different intelligence areas. Although teachers often focus on understanding goals and curricular priorities and do not single out the individual intelligences, they may still find it helpful to examine some of these Internet projects through the lens of multiple intelligences. Some of the Internet projects that pertain to a particular intelligence area are shown in Figure 5.4.

After teachers become familiar with the different types of information exchanges available, they can continue to visit sites to find exchanges that fit into their curriculum standards and understanding goals. Students quickly become motivated when they know that their information will be posted on the Internet for the entire world to see.

Internet-Based Information-Gathering and Analysis Activities		
Information-Gathering and Analysis Activity	**Applicable Curricular Areas**	**Applicable Multiple Intelligences**
Information Exchanges: Classrooms exchange information on topics such as book reviews, weather conditions, family life, sports, and school ecosystems.	language arts science social studies	verbal/linguistic naturalist interpersonal intrapersonal bodily/kinesthetic
Electronic Publishing: Students collect and analyze information and publish newspapers, literary magazines, or electronic journals.	social studies language arts	verbal/linguistic intrapersonal interpersonal
Virtual Field Trips: Students visit locations around the world via the Internet. Expeditions taken by specialists can also be shared.	social studies language arts science music art	visual/spatial interpersonal verbal/linguistic music/rhythmic naturalist
Database Creation: Students collect information and then organize it into a database and graphs for others to use.	science mathematics social studies	logical/mathematical visual/spatial verbal/linguistic interpersonal
Pooled Data Analysis: Students gather data at multiple sites and compare data for numeric or pattern analysis. Students may use a survey or questionnaire.	science mathematics language arts	naturalist verbal/linguistic logical/mathematical

Figure 5.3

Source: Adapted and reprinted with permission from Judi Harris, *Virtual Architecture: Designing and Directing Curriculum-Based Telecomputing,* © 1998 Judi Harris. All rights reserved.

Electronic Publishing

One of the most powerful motivators for writers of any age is to see their work published. Electronic publishing allows students to compose a piece of written work and submit it for publication on any number of Web sites. Many Web sites allow writers to provide feedback to other writers and provide an interactive forum for students to work on their writing. After students spend time on these sites reading other students' stories and poems, teachers can take an opportunity to discuss what makes good writing.

Examples of sites that provide electronic publishing include Comm Tech Lab (www.commtechlab.msu.edu/sites/letsnet/noframes/bigideas/b6/index.html) and Sites for Teachers (www.sitesforteachers.com/resources_sharp/language_arts/la_pub.html). A great site for middle school students is the Midlink Magazine (longwood.cs.ucf.edu/~MidLink), which features articles written by and for middle school students.

Electronic publishing offers students an opportunity to work in their verbal and linguistic intelligences as well as in their personal intelligences. Many students come to school lacking motivation to write. Although they spend years in school writing answers to questions and getting a check or check plus on their papers, they receive very little feedback or comments. As most writers attest, one of the joys of writing is knowing that others will read and enjoy the writer's work. The Internet offers an opportunity to provide this satisfaction to students.

Information Exchange Examples by Multiple Intelligence	
Intelligence	**Information Exchange Example**
Verbal/Linguistic	*Kidwriters Writing Studio* (www.kidlink.org/KIDPROJ/Kidwriters): Students are given abundant exchange opportunities to create and publish original writing for the rest of the world to see.
Logical/Mathematical	*Boiling Points* (astro.uchicago.edu/cara/southpole.edu/boil.html): Students submit the temperature at which water boils at their location to compare with its boiling point at other geographical areas.
Visual/Spatial	*Kid Art* (www.kidlink.org/KIDART): Students study art from around the world and submit their own computer-generated art.
Musical/Rhythmic	*Music Pals* (www.kidlink.org/KIDPROJ/Music): Students study and share the music that influences their lives.
Bodily/Kinesthetic	*Kidnetic* (www.kidnetic.com): A wealth of resources and information exchange about physical fitness. *Get Active Stay Active* (www.getactivestayactive.com): Students keep an activity log to monitor their physical fitness activities.
Interpersonal and Intrapersonal	*Families and Friends* (www.kidlink.org/KIDFORUM/family): Students study different family customs and traditions with students from around the world.
Naturalist	*Historical Trees* (www.nyu.edu/projects/julian/toc.html): Students submit information about a tree of their choice and read about other types of trees.

Figure 5.4

Taking It to the Classroom

What Makes Good Writing Good?

The following activity provides a practical teaching unit on student writing. This can be taught at any grade level and helps students prepare to publish their writing on the Internet.

Brain-Compatibility Link

Focus Links: Choice, Reflection, and Active Learning

In this activity, students are provided with an overview of what makes writing good. They are then given a *choice* of what to write to practice these good writing traits. Students also read other students' writings from different Internet sites and *reflect* on the good and bad writing traits displayed in these pieces. In addition, students become *active learners* by reading and analyzing others' writings, and then writing their own pieces to show their understanding. Teachers do not simply tell students what good writing is, but they involve students in discovering good writing for themselves.

Charting the Way

The preplanning questions help guide the lesson to meet goals and objectives.

Q1. What are the deep understandings of this activity?

Students understand the important components inherent in all good pieces of writing.

Q2. What skills and knowledge, both academic and Internet-based, will students strengthen as a result of this project?

Students are introduced to seven traits of strong writing. Students identify these traits in others' writing examples published on the Internet.

Q3. What facts do students need to become familiar with through this activity?

Good writing includes a majority of the seven traits of good writing.

Q4. How can students' understanding, knowledge, and skills be assessed?

Students are assessed for their understanding of this complex issue through the Understanding Assessment Form shown in Figure 3.3. By using the reproducible blank rubric in Appendix B, teachers can assess how well students explain and interpret what good writing is and how they apply this knowledge with a fresh perspective, empathy, and self-knowledge in their own writing.

Q5. What type of Internet activity will help students reach these learning goals? What will the Internet activity entail? How long will the activity last?

This electronic publishing activity allows students to explore Web sites that publish student writing and analyze writing for the 6+1 Traits of good writing explained on the next two pages. Project duration is approximately three 60-minute sessions.

Q6. What intelligences can be brought into this Internet project to help students gain understanding?

- *Verbal and linguistic:* Students write and analyze the writing of others.
- *Interpersonal:* Students read and respond to others' writing styles.
- *Intrapersonal:* Students analyze their own strengths and weaknesses in writing.

Discovering Internet-Based Resources

The following Web sites offer easy access to student writing, clear instructions on what students need to do to submit their own writing, and enjoyable presentations. These sites are most appropriate for students in Grades 2–8.

- Association for Library Service to Children (www.ala.org/ala/alsc/greatwebsites/greatwebsiteswriting.htm)
- Children's Express (www.childrens-express.org)
- KidsBookshelf (www.kidsbookshelf.com/gsfk/homeworkhelp.asp)
- Kidwriters Writing Studio (www.kidlink.org/KIDPROJ/Kidwriters)

Stepping Out

Teachers use the following steps to guide the lesson process:

1. Lay the groundwork for this activity by having students read a piece of good writing and a piece a poor writing. Ask students what makes writing good writing. Have students brainstorm the traits of a well-written piece.
2. Introduce the following key traits to good writing if they were not already listed. This list of good writing traits comes from the Northwest Regional Educational Laboratory's 6+1 Trait Writing program (www.nwrel.org/assessment/department.php?d=1)[3]:
   a. **Ideas.** Is the writing clear and focused? Does it have a central theme? Does the writer know the subject well? Is the writing filled with important details?
   b. **Organization.** Are there strong links between ideas? Does the beginning of the story invite the reader into it? Does each section of the writing build on what comes before it? Does the reader ever feel lost? Does the conclusion tie up loose ends?
   c. **Voice.** Does the writing sound as if a real person wrote it? Does it have a style and personality? Does it bring the topic to life? Does it make the reader feel something?
   d. **Word Choice.** Does the writer choose the right words? Does the writer use words that are easy to understand and fun to read? Does the writer choose unique and special words?

   e. **Sentence Fluency.** Do sentences vary in length and structure? Do sentences link to previous ideas? Does the paper invite expressive oral reading?
   f. **Conventions.** Does the writing look edited and polished? Does the writing have few mistakes in spelling, punctuation, grammar, capitalization, and paragraphing?
   g. **Presentation.** Is the writing usually pleasing? Is it easy to read and inviting to the reader?

3. Discuss the Understanding Assessment Form to remind students how they will be assessed.

4. Tell students to visit several Web sites that publish student writing. Ask them to read several stories (two to three, depending on length) and reflect on each student's writing by analyzing if the writing displays the 6+1 Traits of good writing.

5. Give students time to write their own stories. Remind them to use the 6+1 Traits.

6. Give students the option of submitting their writing for possible publication on an electronic site.

Virtual Field Trips

One of the first budget cuts made in any school district seems to be funds for field trips. In the past decade, public schools have experienced a steady decline in the number of field trips taken by students and teachers. In the past, teachers and students would climb on a big yellow school bus and be carried to places that expanded students' learning and opened up new worlds. Now the Internet has replaced the big yellow school bus in many districts throughout the nation.

Virtual field trips are the next best thing to being there. These field trips can open doors and windows to experiences and locations from around the world and offer students virtual experiences like they never before encountered. The growing number of virtual field trips is a testimony to their popularity in the classroom. They are popular because they quickly expand a learning experience for students. Because the number of virtual field trip sites has grown, teachers find it rather easy to plan trips that relate directly to their curriculum standards and learning goals.

Many Web sites link teachers and curriculum with virtual field trips. One site is the Virtual Field Trip site (www.geocities.com/CollegePark/Union/2106/fieldtrip.htm), which includes a nice list of trips students and teachers can take. Figure 5.5 gives examples of sites that relate both to curriculum and to specific intelligences.

Teachers must ask themselves how virtual field trips can be used in the curriculum. It is wonderful that students can visit so many different sites and experience places and events. Yet teachers must answer one question before making

Virtual Field Trips by Multiple Intelligence	
Intelligence	**Virtual Field Trip Sites**
Verbal/Linguistic	Classics for Young People (www.ucalgary.ca/~dkbrown/storclas.html) Roald Dahl (www.roalddahlfans.com) Children's Storybooks Online (K–3) (www.magickeys.com/books/index.html)
Logical/Mathematical	MEGA Mathematics (www.c3.lanl.gov/mega-math) The Geometry Center (www.geom.uiuc.edu)
Visual/Spatial	A Hotlist of Virtual Field Trips (www.kn.pacbell.com/wired/fil/pages/listvirtualgr.html) Internet4Classrooms Virtual Field Trips (www.internet4classrooms.com/vft.htm)
Musical/Rhythmic	The Blue Highway (www.thebluehighway.com) Rock and Roll Hall of Fame (www.rockhall.com)
Bodily/Kinesthetic	New York City Ballet (www.nycballet.com) Pow Wow Dancing (www.powwows.com)
Interpersonal and Intrapersonal	Martin Luther King Jr. (seattletimes.nwsource.com/mlk) Neuroscience for Kids (faculty.washington.edu/chudler/neurok.html)
Naturalist	WhaleNet (whale.wheelock.edu/Welcome.html) Carl Hayden Bee Research Center (www.ars.usda.gov/Main/docs.htm?docid=12371) The Bug Club (www.ex.ac.uk/bugclub) Hurricane Storm Science Center (www.miamisci.org/hurricane) Field Guides Center (www.field-guides.com)

Figure 5.5

any decision to use virtual field trips: Will students' learning and understanding of a concept be increased as a result of a virtual field trip? If the field trip is merely an experience, teachers are better off skipping it.

For example, one of the more popular field trips for teachers in Southern California is walking or a short bus trip to tour the beach. Some teachers use this as a time for students to relax, possibly walk through some tide pools, and have a picnic lunch. Yet other teachers visit the tide pools, get on their hands and knees with their students surrounding them, and teach students firsthand about the ocean's incredible ecosystem. Many of these students experience the beach as a classroom for the first time, and they approach the experience full of wonder and excitement.

Similarly, a virtual field trip can simply be an experience for students—a place to visit and stay a little while—or it can be a wonderful and exciting learning opportunity. In the hands of teachers who have direct goals and objectives for what they want students to learn, virtual field trips open a world of wonder and excitement. The teacher's job is to select a series of virtual field trips that provide a broad range of information and experiences on the same general theme or concept. This provides an added punch to a lesson that studying from a textbook simply cannot offer. Teachers should use virtual field trips to broaden and deepen the learning experience for students, not to teach facts.

The Virtual Field Trip Ticket (Figure 5.6) provides an example of how teachers can organize these trips within their existing curriculum and hold students accountable for their travels. Some teachers ask students to use field journals throughout the year to complete activities and reflect upon trips taken on the Internet. This journal idea is appropriate when teachers use virtual field trips frequently during the year and want to provide opportunities for students to practice their verbal/linguistic intelligence skills as they express opinions and thoughts in writing. Journals also provide students a good place for self-reflection, fostering metacognition and transfer of learning.

Taking It to the Classroom

Virtual Field Trips

Virtual field trips can be motivating and challenging experiences for students. In the hands of teachers who have direct goals and objectives for what they want students to learn, these adventures broaden lessons and deepen knowledge. The teacher's job is to select a series of virtual field trips that provide information and experiences about an important curriculum topic. Virtual field trips add spice to lessons, because they involve students in actively seeking and creating their own knowledge.

The example used in this activity is the United States Civil War. Many students learn about the Civil War each year, but the war becomes much more meaningful and personal for students when they take virtual field trips that engage their multiple intelligences. Before starting this project, students should have a basic knowledge base about the Civil War—why the war was fought, where the battles took place, and what the outcome of the war entailed. Teachers should review basic knowledge before starting, if necessary.

Virtual Field Trip Ticket

You have been invited to attend a virtual field trip where you will visit several different places. It is always a good idea to plan a trip carefully before you start. You are to keep a field notebook in which you will reflect on each trip and answer questions regarding your visits.

The theme for this series of field trips is ____________________

Your itinerary for your field trip includes:

Web site	URL Address
____________________	____________________
____________________	____________________
____________________	____________________

Choose two of the following three assignments to complete for your field journal:

1. *Summary:* Write a summary detailing what each site had to offer and what you learned about the topic.

2. *Mind Map:* Draw a mind map. Write the common theme of the field trips in the middle of the page and connect what you learned at each site to this central theme in a way that organizes the information that you learned.

3. *Web site:* Design your own virtual field trip Web site about this topic. Create the first Web page with links to additional pages. Clearly outline what content the attached pages include about the topic.

Figure 5.6

Brain-Compatibility Link

Focus Links: Meaning and Relevance, Emotions, Prior Knowledge

It is not easy to interest students in a war that occurred long ago. For most students, the U.S. Civil War seems irrelevant and meaningless. Yet, this activity seeks to add both *meaning* and *relevance* by asking students to visit sites that have pictures, personal accounts, and other human interest information. By doing so, students receive *emotional* content within their study of the Civil War. In addition, this lesson is designed to build on students' *prior knowledge*.

Charting the Way

The preplanning questions help guide the lesson to meet goals and objectives.

Q1. What are the deep understandings of this activity?

Students come to a deeper understanding of the causes and effects of the Civil War. Students gain an understanding of the human experience of this war.

Q2. What skills and knowledge, both academic and Internet-based, will students strengthen as a result of this activity?

Students gain knowledge and information about the Civil War.
Students practice finding and using information from the Internet.
Students learn how to access and use Web sites that offer virtual field trip experiences.

Q3. What facts do students need to become familiar with through this activity?

Students learn about the causes and locations of the Civil War.
Students learn who won the war and at what cost.

Q4. How can students' understanding, knowledge, and skills be assessed?

The Understanding Rubric (Figure 3.4 and in Appendix B) provides a valuable assessment tool for teachers and students. By using the rubric, teachers assess how well students can explain and understand major concepts about the Civil War and apply this knowledge with a fresh perspective, empathy, and self-knowledge.

Students complete two separate activities using the information received from their field trip experiences. These activities should display students' growing depth of knowledge about the Civil War. Learning facts and dates is not as important as understanding why this war happened and how it has influenced every American's life.

Q5. What type of Internet activity will help students reach these learning goals? What will the Internet activity entail? How long will the activity last?

Students participate in virtual field trips to gain information about the Civil War. Students complete activities based on their information. The project requires approximately three 60-minute sessions.

Q6. What intelligences can be brought into this Internet activity to help students gain understanding?

- *Verbal and linguistic:* Students access information via Web site readings.
- *Visual and spatial:* Students study maps and battle strategies on Web sites and create mind maps regarding the Civil War.
- *Interpersonal:* Students work with partners to design Web sites.

Discovering Internet-Based Resources

The following Web sites can serve as virtual field trips back in time to the Civil War. These sites allow students to learn about the Civil War using several intelligences. In addition, these sites are rich with details and experiences and lead to other sites for students to explore on their virtual field trip. There are literally hundreds of Web sites about the Civil War that can be used for this activity, but these sites represent a good sampling of what is available.

- The Valley of the Shadow (valley.vcdh.virginia.edu)
- Selected Civil War Photographs (www.memory.loc.gov/ammem/cwphtml/cwphome.html)
- The United States Civil War Center (www.cwc.lsu.edu)

Stepping Out

Teachers use the following steps to guide the lesson process.

1. Discuss the concept of virtual field trips and when and why they are used.
2. Explain to students that this activity is an extension of what the class has already been learning about the Civil War. Explain that they are going on a field trip back in time to the Civil War. The purpose of the virtual field trip is to add to their experiences, to broaden those experiences to increase understanding of a concept, and to deepen their learning and understanding about this time in history.

3. Pair students and hand out a United States Civil War virtual field trip ticket based on Figure 5.6. Explain that they will visit specific sites to learn more about the Civil War.
4. Discuss the assessment process by going over the Understanding Rubric (Figure 3.4 and in Appendix B).
5. Ask student pairs to choose two concluding activities that relate to their new information.
   a. **Summary.** Write a summary detailing what each site had to offer and what you learned about the topic. With a partner, read and edit one another's summary before turning them in as final products.
   b. **Mind Map.** Draw a mind map with the common theme of the field trips in the middle of the page and what was learned at each site connected to this central theme in a way that organizes the information learned. With a partner, read and offer suggestions about one another's mind map before turning them in as final products.
   c. **Web site.** With a partner, design a virtual filed trip Web site about this topic. Create the first Web page with links to additional pages. Clearly outline what content the attached pages would include about the topic.
6. Give students time to visit sites, explore the information, and work on activities.
7. Ask students to share their final products with another set of partners, if time allows.

Database Creation

Some Internet projects involve collecting information and organizing it into databases and graphs for others to use. These activities require students to use several key information literacy skills in collecting, organizing, analyzing, and sharing information. Many of these projects are ongoing and long-lasting. Examples of database projects can be found on the Kidlink site (www.kidlink.org).

One particular example on this site is a multicultural calendar where students from around the world have contributed to a database that includes holidays celebrated where they live. Another example is the Global Grocery List Project (www.gsn.org/GSH/project/gg) where classes gather information on grocery prices and then compare and analyze the data using a database format.

When would a database creation project be useful in a classroom? How can a project like this be helpful to student understanding and learning? Database creation projects can be used to help students recognize the scope and variety of things throughout the world. For example, it is quite easy for students to see only their environment, their ecosystem, and their way of life, but database creation projects help students recognize the large amount and variety of cultural traditions throughout the world. Through these projects, students use their interpersonal and intrapersonal intelligences within a specific curriculum area, helping them understand and accept the diversity of the world and its people and making them aware of their own place in this changing world. Many teachers use database creation projects to enhance their math curriculum, providing engaging applications to concepts such as averages, means, and scattergrams.

Pooled Data Analysis

Pooled data analysis activities require students to gather data at multiple sites and combine it for numeric and/or pattern analysis. Data collection usually takes the form of a survey or questionnaire. Students create surveys about a subject that they can send to others through the Internet. As responses are received, students collect and analyze the data and eventually post the final analysis on the Internet for all to see.

Students may participate in a simple pooled data analysis project by collecting data on environmental conditions, such as the number of days it rains in different places across the nation or the type of animals commonly seen by students in different geographical locations. This type of electronic data collection and analysis makes subjects come alive for students and motivates them to understand concepts so that they might report their findings and analysis to an audience outside of their classroom.

Many good pooled data analysis projects exist on the Internet and are open for teachers to examine and possibly join. For example, the Marvelous M&M Project (teams.lacoe.edu/documentation/projects/math/mm.html) allows students to share the colors of their M&M's from one bag and tally and report totals. The Kidlympics site (www.kidlink.org/KIDPROJ/Kidlympics) is a good physical education project because it has students compete in certain physical fitness events and submit their results.

Information-gathering and analysis projects provide students with engaging applications of the concepts and ideas they are being challenged to understand. It is easy for students to fake understanding of a concept by sitting quietly in a large classroom and returning memorized facts at the appropriate times. When students are required to show their understanding in real-world applications, teachers can truly assess student understanding and identify the instructional needs of the students. By providing information-gathering and analysis projects while students constantly strengthen their information literacy skills, teachers engage and empower students in their quest for understanding.

6

Improving Questioning and Problem-Solving Skills

Teachers often find it difficult to consistently fit active participation, time, and discussion into their lessons. Even teachers who work with the Understanding by Design lesson format and create Internet-based activities begin to realize that, although they want to get their students to really understand a concept, it is difficult to include all of these consistently into their lessons. Teachers want to give their students time to explore concepts, work with information, and gain a deeper understanding of the issues, but it is very difficult to do it in a system that values covering a lot of material at surface level. Yet if teachers want their students to leave each spring with deeper understandings of a few concepts, several techniques can help them reach this goal. This chapter explores the technique of using questioning to guide instruction and learning and presents problem-solving Internet activities as classroom activities to practice this technique.

UNCOVERAGE

A familiar topic of conversation in staff lounges throughout the nation is the discussion between covering a topic briefly versus teaching a concept in depth. In this day and age of standards, teachers feel pressure to teach a lot of information quickly. Yet it is important for teachers to recognize that going in depth into a topic is critical for students to engage in learning and to help them really understand important and complex topics.

According to Wiggins and McTighe (1998/2005), "When we 'cover' material, we end up unwittingly focusing on the surface details, without going into depth on any of them. From the learner's perspective, everything appears of equal value—a bunch of facts to be remembered, with no hierarchy, memorable priority, or connected meanings" (p. 229).

Instead of just covering material, teachers need to provide lessons that allow students to "uncover" the material—to directly experience the inquiries, arguments, and applications of the subject. As Wiggins and McTighe (1998/2005) explain, "To uncover something, by contrast, suggests finding something important in what has become hidden—to reveal rather than conceal" (p. 230).

To provide deeper learning experiences, teachers can provide extensions, connections, and links to each Internet-based activity, allowing students to understand how concepts relate to other concepts. The Internet is especially helpful to teachers trying to help students connect the dots in their learning—to see that certain events relate to other seemingly irrelevant events. This happens by clicking the mouse on Web site links that relate in one way or another to the information presented on the site.

Many Internet sites include a similar amount of surface knowledge about a subject as textbooks present. Therefore, students rarely gain a further depth or breadth of understanding by simply visiting an array of Web sites. Understanding is enhanced only if the teacher designs an Internet activity that allows meaning and relevance to be brought to life. Teachers might say to students, Here is a problem or dilemma. What do you think? One technique teachers can use in conjunction with Internet-based learning activities is to pose questions that help guide students to what they need to learn and understand.

QUESTIONING

Questions help learning activities come to life with relevance and challenge. However, questions come in all shapes and sizes. Teachers must identify what types of questions they need to ask to further student understanding of content matter and to help students use their multiple intelligences in their quest for answers and understanding.

Fat or Skinny Questions?

Fogarty (2001), in *Brain-Compatible Classrooms*, distinguished fat from skinny questions. This simplified way of looking at questioning can easily be shared with students and parents. *Fat questions* ask *how* or *why* and require reasoning and justification to support an answer. *Skinny questions* can be answered with yes, no, or a one-word answer.

When teachers ask fat questions, they require students to use higher-order thinking skills based on discussion and explanation. These questions take time to think through and, in many cases, require research and reading to find a reply or answer. There is no rote answer to fat questions—as Fogarty put it, "Fat questions get fat answers."

Skinny questions, however, require very little thinking or discussing and not much time is needed to formulate an answer. Skinny questions ask students to list answers or simply provide pieces of information back without having to use the information. Skinny questions get skinny answers.

Essential, Unit, and Entry-Point Questions

Wiggins and McTighe (1998/2005) labeled questions as the "doorways to understanding" and encouraged educators to use questions that help students uncover material as they seek understanding. They ask educators to design lessons by building curriculum and activities around questions that are fundamental to concepts and content matter. By using questions in this way, activities and units can be more focused and organized for inquiry. Questions help connect seemingly disconnected pieces of information and learning activities—students focus on finding answers to overarching questions rather than simply completing an activity.

Teachers can also take specific content or performance standards and turn them into questions. For example, if the content standard for fifth grade social studies reads, "Students will understand the reasons for western expansion," a teacher could ask students at the beginning of the unit why so many people leave the comforts of eastern settlements to travel west and start all over again. The teachers can then design assessments and learning activities based around this large concept, and students can focus on finding answers to this complex question. This approach differs greatly from the approach of a teacher standing in front of the class lecturing on the five top reasons settlers moved west.

Wiggins and McTighe (1998/2005) identified different types of questions that can be used to guide instruction, assessment, and activities—essential, topical, and entry-point questions are a few that can be used with students. Teachers can create problem-solving Internet activities that help students develop answers to these probing questions.

Essential questions are complex, thought-provoking, and have no one right or pat answer. They lead students into lively discussions, debates, and even arguments as they illuminate a subject's complexity and controversies. Asked at the beginning of a unit of study, essential questions are broad, overarching questions that guide students into inquiry and research. Essential questions have the following characteristics:

1. They cause genuine and relevant inquiry into the big ideas and core content.
2. They provoke deep thought, lively discussion, sustained inquiry, and new understanding, as well as more questions.
3. They require students to consider alternatives, weigh evidence, and support their ideas and justify their answers.

4. They stimulate vital, ongoing rethinking of big ideas, assumptions, and prior lessons.

5. They spark meaningful connections with prior learning and personal experiences.

6. They naturally recur, creating opportunities for transfer to other situations and subjects. (Wiggins & McTighe, 1998/2005, p. 110)

By using essential questions, teachers can motivate students to think and problem solve. When it becomes obvious that there is no one right answer and that disagreement and controversy may be involved, student interest is usually piqued. Many times, essential questions give rise to other important questions, which help students learn about the relationship between subjects and concepts.

Some examples of essential questions might include:

- Is the Internet dangerous?
- In the natural world, do only the strong survive?
- Does music reflect culture or help shape it?
- What makes a great book?
- Does the invention of new technologies always lead to progress?

Unit Topical questions are more subject specific and can be used to frame or scaffold a particular content or a curricular area. They provide an entry point into a specific lesson or content area and lead students into related essential questions. Topical questions usually do not have one obviously right answer and can be used to start student discussions and pique student interest. The line between unit and essential questions is not black and white, but instead, these types of questions lay on a continuum of specificity. Topical questions can be a type of essential question, leading students into even broader essential questions.

Examples of unit questions might include:

- What is the moral of the story in *The Red Badge of Courage*?
- Why is Mexico City located where it is?
- Is the Independent Counsel position justifiable?
- How do organisms survive in harsh or changing environments?

Entry-point questions link students' daily lives and interests to the bigger concepts and understandings teachers want students to learn. They can act as a doorway into these other questions. Essential or topic questions are not the best jumping off point for beginning a unit or course of study when the material itself is not relevant to students' daily life. For example, it might be difficult to get students initially interested in a study of slavery with essential questions such as, Is slavery always wrong? or Is there current-day slavery in America? Although student interest might eventually join in without an initial discussion, it is difficult for students to immediately warm up to these broad questions. In this situation, teachers might use an entry-point question to stir student interest with controversy by asking if having children do chores is a form of slavery. A lively discussion will most likely follow and lead the class into the unit of study and the essential questions.

PROBLEM-SOLVING ACTIVITIES

Teachers can use a question-answer-question cycle to guide lesson designs. A natural extension of this cycle is problem-solving activities that can be designed around questions and provide opportunities for students to gather information and develop answers to questions using the Internet as their base of operation. Many unit, essential, or fat questions require students to gather, analyze, synthesize, and evaluate information as they form intelligent answers to the questions posed or create solutions to problems.

Problem-solving Internet-based activities represent a powerful way to use the Internet with students. In her article "Tools for the Mind," author Mary Burn (2006) states,

> In addition to lower-order tools, classrooms use more robust tools, such as the Internet, in such nondifferentiated ways that they dilute their power. Although students use the Internet to access information, I have seen little evidence of students engaging in more complex and dynamic kinds of online learning opportunities—such as online collaboration or content-oriented simulations—despite the fact that much of the rationale for broadband access in schools was for students to take part in such opportunities. (p. 50)

To escape these passive, copy-and-paste type of instructional activities, teachers can use problem-based learning activities. In many classrooms, problem-based learning provides real-world learning experiences for students to find relevance and meaning in specific curricular areas.

Problem-Based Learning

Problem-based learning is a curriculum model that uses real-world problems structured to be open-ended. Many times, the problem presents a complex situation with no obvious solution. Problem-based learning is a powerful technique because it engages students in relevant and meaningful inquiry and provides them with a sense of empowerment in their own learning and problem-solving capabilities. This teaching model can be used throughout the curriculum and works nicely with the questioning techniques mentioned previously. In addition, problems can be approached through the lens of multiple intelligences.

Fogarty (1997) offers several steps that can be used in problem-based learning. Teachers will quickly recognize the direct relationship between problem-based learning and the information literacy skills defined in Chapter 5. This is an important link—solving problems by handling and working well with information is truly a twenty-first-century basic skill. The recommended steps for problem-based learning are as follows:

1. *Define the problem.* Students gain an understanding of the problem and state it in their own words. Students identify what they know and need to know to solve the problem.
2. *Identify final assessment.* Students are told how they will be assessed in the final analysis. Rubrics, classroom assessments, final projects or assignments, or tests can be used in any combination. It is important that students know what is expected from them as they solve the problem.
3. *Gather the facts.* Students tap into their prior knowledge and use their multiple intelligences to find information related to the problem.
4. *Hypothesize.* Students use their logical/mathematical intelligence to begin to hypothesize about the problem.
5. *Research.* Students use the Internet and other resources to research data and gather more information. Students can also use the Multiple Intelligences Information-Gathering Suggestions (Figure 5.2) as a guide in their research.
6. *Rephrase the problem.* As their research continues, students rephrase the problem statement to reflect new information, allowing the problem to become more specific.
7. *Generate alternatives.* Students generate many alternatives and then eventually select the best solution. If students are working in a group, their interpersonal intelligence can be tapped to become a part of a problem-solving team. Teams create lists of alternative solutions to the problem.
8. *Advocate solutions.* Students justify the solution they feel is best to other team members and in their final project or assessment.

Students can practice these problem-based learning strategies in several different types of problem-solving Internet activities (see Figure 6.1). These activities also provide opportunities for students to wrestle with big questions posed at the beginning of the activity.

Many of these problem-solving activities provide students with ongoing practice in searching for and using information to solve problems in a real-world setting. These activities ask students to search out information for a myriad of reasons—to solve a problem, to research a topic, or to participate in a telecollaborative activity. Keeping these main purposes in mind, teachers can use a myriad of Internet problem-solving activities to provide students with practice in their information-searching skills and in using information in a real-world setting. Teachers may find it a little more challenging to locate collaborative problem-solving activities that link directly to their curriculum. Yet as participation in K–12 classrooms grows, the variety and subject matter of problem-solving activities continue to broaden.

Information Searches

Information searches are presented as either collaborative or competitive activities in which students are given information and clues, and then use reference sources (either on or off the Internet) to answer questions. Information searches can be designed as independent class activities or as interactive processes. At times, a teacher will pose a unit or essential question to students, provide a few clues and key pieces of information, and let students work independently or in small groups to find information and develop an answer. At other times, a teacher will find an information search competition on the Internet that pertains to a specific unit of study and enroll his or her students in that information search game.

When considering information searches, teachers need to recognize the main reasons and motivations of searching for information in the first place. Harris (1998) identifies six main purposes for students to seek out information:

1. *Practice information-seeking skills.* This practice includes using the Internet searching skills mentioned in Chapter 4, learning to work efficiently with search engines, and improving search skills within specific Web sites.

2. *Become informed about a topic of inquiry and/or answer a question.* Many Internet activities are geared toward helping students find information to answer a question or research a topic. Information-searching activities assist students in this direction.

3. *Review multiple perspectives on an issue.* One of the great benefits of students working on the Internet is the accessibility to multiple perspectives on issues. When students read a textbook, one perspective is provided; but when they search for information on the Internet, multiple perspectives can be found. This helps students learn that issues are more complex and complicated than they may appear on the surface.

4. *Generate data needed to explore a topic.* The Internet can help students participate in real research and studies and generate data they can use as they explore a topic. For example, students can be a part of sea exploration and may even go as far as controlling a robotic arm on a marine biology boat via the Internet.

5. *Solve authentic problems.* A major tenet of constructivist learning is providing students with opportunities to explore and find solutions to real-world and meaningful problems. The Internet provides these opportunities by bringing authentic problems into the classroom setting.

6. *Publish synthesized and/or critiqued information overviews for other students to use.* More and more students and classrooms throughout the world publish their research and work for the others to see and use. This is an important use for the Internet because classrooms can build on one another's knowledge base instead of starting from scratch. (pp. 66–76)

An example of an information-search activity in which students become informed about a topic is the Global SchoolNet's Geogame (www.gsn.org/GSH/project/gg). This site asks classes to submit ten pieces of information about their school's location based on key geographic categories. The class then receives other classrooms' hints and uses geographical resources to find where in the United States the other classrooms are located.

Problem-Solving Activities		
Problem-Solving Activity	**Applicable Curricular Areas**	**Applicable Multiple Intelligences**
Information searches: Students are provided with clues and use the Internet and other references to solve problems.	science social studies	verbal/linguistic naturalist logical/mathematical
Peer feedback: Students post writings and other projects on the Internet with the purpose of receiving feedback from peers.	language arts social studies	verbal/linguistic interpersonal intrapersonal
Parallel problem solving: A similar problem is presented to students in several locations that they solve separately at each site. They then share problem-solving methods and answers.	science mathematics social studies	logical/mathematical naturalist interpersonal intrapersonal
Simulations: Students participate in collaborative projects that simulate specific activities and events (e.g., a simulated space shuttle launch that uses person-to-person communication to create the simulated situation).	science social studies language arts	verbal/linguistic interpersonal
Social action projects: Students work on a project with other classrooms that centers on a social issue. For example, classrooms might study pollution and choose a specific day to have a community clean up.	social studies science	interpersonal intrapersonal verbal/linguistic naturalist
Sequential creations: A group of students begins a project or writing piece and sends it to another class so that they can add to the creation.	language arts social studies	verbal/linguistic interpersonal
Telepresent problem solving: Activities bring together students from different geographical locations in real time to participate in a virtual meeting or do similar activities at the same time.	social studies language arts science	interpersonal verbal/linguistic

Figure 6.1

Source: Adapted and reprinted with permission from Judi Harris, *Virtual Architecture: Designing and Directing Curriculum-Based Telecomputing*,

This type of information search activity can be an exciting fit for the geography curriculum when a teacher wants students to learn about time zones, latitude and longitude, land formations, and other key geography concepts. If the teacher starts with the unit question, What makes Smith Town unique?, students are off and running as they identify unique qualities, learn about the geographical identities of Smith Town, and then share these traits with the rest of the nation. In addition, students apply their learning about geography to find the locations of other schools using geographical and other clues. This type of problem-solving activity is also an excellent way to help students use and strengthen their naturalist intelligence as they turn their focused attention to critical details of the environment in which they live.

Another excellent Web site for information searches is the WebQuest Page (webquest.sdsu.edu). This award-winning site was developed at San Diego State University. A WebQuest is an inquiry-oriented activity in which most or all of the information used by learners is drawn from the Web. WebQuests are designed to use learners' time well because students focus on using information rather than looking for it.

In addition, students are challenged to think at the higher levels of analysis, synthesis, and evaluation. Activities provide an interesting task or problem that requires students to actively search for information and then use that information to draw conclusions, complete the task, or solve the problem. This well-designed Web site provides WebQuests categorized by primary, upper elementary, and middle school ages. Examples of WebQuest activities include learning about endangered animals, researching and learning about the sun, and studying the life of Anne Frank. Each WebQuest is created using the same sequence: introduction, task, process and resources, and conclusion.

Peer Feedback

A peer feedback Internet activity asks students to post writings and other projects on the Internet so that they might receive feedback from peers. Peers from around the nation—and even the world—offer constructive responses and comments to others' work. These responses might range from comments on the writer's ideas to critiques on how the piece of writing or project is constructed. For example, the KidPub Web site (www.kidpub.com/kidpub) offers a very easy format for students to submit their stories and add paragraphs to other student stories, and it ranks the stories in order of popularity with readers.

Before students participate in a peer feedback activity, teachers need to discuss the purpose of feedback and the different types students can provide to their peers. Students should be taught to "sandwich" their feedback by beginning with a positive statement, offering constructive comments on how to improve the piece, and ending with a positive statement. Students practice giving feedback to peers in their classroom before trying it online.

Parallel Problem Solving

Parallel problem solving as an Internet activity is very popular, because it poses a problem to several groups of students in different locations and all groups share problem-solving methods and answers. An example is the What Is

EnergyNet site (www.energynet.net/eninfo/info/what_is_energynet.html), which poses the question to classrooms, Is your school wasting energy? This site helps students find answers by providing the technical support and telecommunications tools they need. Along the way, students are given opportunities to work on their team-building, problem-solving, and technical skills. Another example is the Math Forum site (www.mathforum.org) that provides math problems, solutions to those problems, and other information and discussions.

Parallel problem-solving activities also offer teachers and students an opportunity to design their own Internet activity and post it on the Internet for others to participate. For example, a teacher might start a curriculum unit with the question, Are there times when the president should be above the law? Using this unit question as a guide, a class can design a Web site that raises the question and links to several times in history when a president made a decision to participate in a shady or illegal act for what he perceived was a benefit for the country (e.g., Iran-Contra Affair, Watergate, etc.). Students invite other classrooms to participate in this parallel problem-solving activity through research and discussion before submitting their opinion on the subject. By using the Internet in this way, student perspectives and critical thinking skills can be broadened through exposure to other students' research and opinions.

Simulations

Simulations are collaborative Internet projects that simulate specific activities and events for students. They are the next best thing to being there. Students can learn what it is like to fly the space shuttle or to correspond with George Washington.

One site that offers ongoing simulations and is worth a teacher's bookmark is Educational Simulations (www.simulations.com). This site asks students to simulate founding their own country—from developing a government and constitution, through creating an economic and judicial system. Another simulation offered through this site is what it has been like to be in a school near the Panama Canal. It offers classrooms and students an opportunity for in-depth study of the Panama Canal area.

Another excellent simulation for middle and high school social studies is the Rivertown Simulation (www.emich.edu/public/geo/rtownintro.html). Rivertown is a fictitious town undergoing revitalization. This project is a group effort and involves students in making decisions about how to revitalize the run-down town with new input. This educational simulation is an excellent activity for a curriculum focused on local and civic government, community issues, or group decision making. Students use their interpersonal, visual and spatial, and logical and mathematical intelligences as they grapple with financial and social issues related to downtown revitalization.

A superb high school simulation that relates to social studies and math is the National Budget Simulation (www.budgetsim.org/nbs). This simulation asks students to balance the national budget by cutting or adding to specific social and military programs. Students use their logical and mathematical, interpersonal, and verbal and linguistic intelligences to solve national dilemmas revolving around the national budget. This simulation opens students' eyes to the complexity surrounding budget issues as they pertain to society and social issues.

Social Action Projects

In social action projects, students within their classrooms or with other classrooms work on a project that centers on a social issue. For example, classrooms might study the effects of pollution and choose a specific day to have a community clean up.

Many Web sites and Internet projects relate to social action topics. The real power in these activities is providing students with opportunities to be aware of and strengthen their personal and naturalist intelligences. For example, the Greenpeace Web site (www.greenpeace.org) provides students with several different social action causes that Greenpeace is currently concerned about.

Another well-designed site for social action projects and ideas is Envirolink (www.envirolink.org). This site lists social action problems and offers suggestions as to how readers can become involved. Students can begin on this site when they are asked to find a social action problem they feel strongly about. The Green: Global Rivers Environmental Education Network (www.earthforce.org/section/programs/green) gives students opportunities to write an action plan and strategize for social action related to local problems or issues concerning water.

The list of social action issues on the Internet is growing each day. Nonprofit organizations have found the Internet to be a level playing field, because they are now able to present their concerns and call for action on their Web sites. Teachers can give students a list of social action issues to choose from and ask them to use the Internet to research the topic. Students work collaboratively with their classmates and online peers to complete an activity related to that social issue.

Teachers need to remember that social action Internet activities must relate to something they want students to learn or understand. Social action activities relate particularly well to the science and social studies curriculum and can be used nicely with essential, unit, and entry-level questions. A few examples of issues that students can focus on and examples of questions that can guide their inquiry are shown in Figure 6.2. In addition, a classroom activity that focuses on social action follows.

Taking It to the Classroom

Social Action Project

This activity uses the steps of problem-based learning to guide students through a complex social action project related to the rapid growth of development and building in all areas of the United States. The activity begins with a unit question, What price do Americans pay for continued development? This serves as the overarching question throughout the activity.

Social Action Questions and Issues	
Question	**Issue**
Who is responsible for the health of the atmosphere?	Atmosphere crisis: EPA and ozone depletion
What are the consequences of global warming?	Global warming
Does crime ever pay?	Crime
Should society even try to prevent individuals from becoming drug abusers, or is it an individual decision?	Drug abuse and prevention
How has the definition of the term *family* changed in the past 10 years?	Family
Is there more than one way to define *starvation?*	Starvation
How many people can the world support and still be able to function?	Overpopulation
How many different forms of pollution exist?	Pollution
What rights should all humans have regardless of their nationality, gender, or race?	Human rights around the world
Who is responsible for helping the poor?	Poverty

Figure 6.2

Brain-Compatibility Link

Focus Links: Choice, Reflection, and Active Learning

In this activity, students are presented with a problem that relates to their future lives. Within the activity, students *choose* a problem area within development and population growth that they would like to study. This choice increases motivation and adds meaning to students' studies. In addition, students are given time to *reflect* with group members and classmates as they present their findings.

This activity uses *active learning* to make an issue come alive. Although most Internet activities might be classified as active learning, teachers must be aware that active learning is more than simply finding information on the Internet. Active learning entails doing something with that information.

Charting the Way

The preplanning questions help guide the lesson to meet goals and objectives.

Q1. What are the deep understandings of this activity?

Students gain an understanding of the effects of continued development on natural resources.

Q2. What skills and knowledge, both academic and Internet-based, will students strengthen as a result of this activity?

Students strengthen their problem-solving skills.

Students use the Internet for research and to strengthen their searching and information literacy skills.

Q3. What facts do students need to become familiar with through this activity?

Students learn about development and its relationship to natural resources.

Students learn the staggering rate of population growth and the problems that arise because of this growth.

Q4. How can students' understanding, knowledge, and skills be assessed?

Students can be assessed for their understanding of this complex issue through the Understanding Rubric (Figure 3.4 and in Appendix B). Teachers use this rubric to assess how well students can explain and interpret the influence of development and how well they apply this knowledge with a fresh perspective, empathy, and self-knowledge. Teachers should look for students' ability to grasp the complex issues surrounding population growth and the influence of that growth on everything from society to natural resources to social services.

Q5. What type of Internet activity will help students reach these learning goals? What will the Internet activity entail? How long will the activity last?

Students use their information-gathering and analysis Internet skills to complete this activity. This activity uses approximately four 60-minute sessions.

Q6. What intelligences can be brought into this Internet activity to help students gain understanding?

- *Verbal* and *linguistic:* Students access written information about development.
- *Interpersonal:* Students discuss the role of development with others and work in groups.
- *Logical* and *mathematical:* Students calculate the effects of development relative to population growth, natural resource costs, and so forth.
- *Naturalist:* Students research influence on environment and the natural resources needed to sustain population growth.

Discovering Internet-Based Resources

The following Web sites assist students and teachers in their research on development. These sites were selected because they discuss issues surrounding growing population and diminishing natural resources. In addition, there are hundreds of environmental sites that older students should be encouraged to explore to learn more about these issues.

- Facing the Future (www.facingthefuture.org)
- About.com (www.environment.about.com)
- Negative Population Growth (www.npg.org)

Stepping Out

Teachers use the following steps to guide the lesson process.

1. Discuss the issues surrounding growing population and development in the world. Begin by discussing the continued development in the United States. Ask students to bring examples of development (e.g., growth of superstores, sprawling suburbs, etc.).
2. Explain the activity to the students. Tell students they have been hired by a nonprofit company to address a very serious question: What is the price Americans pay for continued development? It seems more and more houses and buildings are being built in the United States and very few people are concerned about what development might do to natural resources and the quality of life. Tell students that, in teams, they will research this issue on the Internet and develop a well-grounded case about why development should be stopped or why it should be allowed to continue.
3. Review the Understanding Rubric (Figure 3.4 and in Appendix B) so students will know how they are to be assessed and what is expected of them.
4. Divide students into teams. Ask students to complete the following six problem-solving stages.
   a. *Define the problem.* What is the problem being addressed within the broader issue of development? For example, what about overpopulation, natural resources, pollution, quality of life in the suburbs, and so forth?
   b. *Gather the facts.* Research the problem on the Internet and use other resources to gain information about the social issue surrounding development.
   c. *Hypothesize.* Make a hypothesis about the problem. For example, possible hypotheses might include: many people will end up homeless without adequate housing and more development or natural resources will be exhausted by the year 2030 with the pace of current development.

   d. *Research and rephrase.* Continue researching and seeking information based on the hypothesis and rephrase the problem as you find more information and your understanding of the issue deepens.
   e. *Generate alternatives.* Create a list of alternatives or suggestions regarding development as it relates to the problem. For example, one alternative is to limit how many children couples can have.
   f. *Advocate solutions.* Be prepared to justify the solutions to the problems to members of the local city government interested in these issues.

5. Ask students to share their findings and results with the class. Consider asking students to make 10-minute presentations of their research, hypotheses, alternatives, and eventual solutions with justifications. Remind them to address the original question, What is the price Americans pay for continued development?

Sequential Creations

In sequential creation activities, groups of students begin a project or piece of writing, send it to another class, and the other class either adds to the creation or posts it on a Web site for others to make additions. An excellent example is the Kids' Space Web site (www.kids-space.org/story/story.html), where students can submit their own writing for publication as well as read other students' writings on the electronic bookshelf. The Writer's Corner Café (www.mv.com/Writers Corner/Homepage.html) asks students to participate in monthly real-time chats during which they put together a story online and are able to contribute as much or little as they want. ZuZu (www.zuzu.org) allows students to share their published writing as well as accompanying artwork or pictures.

Just as with parallel problem-solving activities, a teacher may choose to post sequential creation activities on a Web site and ask other classrooms to participate. For example, a teacher may choose to invite their Keypal class to collaborate on a nonfiction writing assignment about Ben Franklin. Both classes research this famous man and add to an essay posted on the classroom Web site. Sequential creations do not need to be complex. Teachers can begin with simple ideas that are already part of the classroom and ask others to participate and add to the assignment. Doing a sequential creation broadens students' perspectives of a subject and offers livelier peer discussions.

Telepresent Problem Solving

Telepresent problem-solving activities bring students together in real time from different geographical locations to participate in virtual meetings or do similar activities at the same time. These activities are complex and require strong technological knowledge and appropriate technological hardware and software, but they are becoming more common as the hardware and software continue to develop.

For example, a decade ago, the CU-SeeMe program and technology helped teachers make telepresent conversations and problem-solving tasks happen between groups of students. This technology is still used in classrooms and offices today and continues to evolve. At the same time, as Internet bandwidth increases, video conferencing is also emerging as a future technology for schools. Although years away, some day students in a classroom will simply turn on a television and camera and be involved in face-to-face conversations with experts, other classrooms, and people around the world.

A few sample online problem-solving activities are highlighted on Harris's In the Kitchen—Designs for Telecollaboration and Telepresence Web site (virtual-architecture.wm.edu/Telecollaboration/index.html). One of these includes the NASA K–12 Virtual Conferences (www.isoc.org/inet97/proceedings/A5/A5_2.HTM), where students can view a specific NASA activity, ask questions, and discuss ideas with scientists involved in the project.

Another excellent example is the Scholastic Web site (teacher.scholastic.com) that schedules authors of some of the most current and popular children's books for online chats. During the chats, students and teachers can meet and pose questions regarding writing, the books, and other pertinent topics. A powerful feature of these types of Internet sites is the ability for teachers to pose a unit or entry-level question that students can then address and discuss with the featured speaker.

Problem-solving activities allow students an interactive opportunity to strengthen their problem-solving skills in a real-world context. As students are directed through essential, unit, and entry-level questions, these Internet activities take on focus and meaning relative to the curriculum. There is nothing more motivating for students than to discuss and solve real-world problems.

Appendix A

Web Site Addresses

Site Name	Comments	URL
4Teachers	Explains how each intelligence is used in writing	www.4teachers.org
6+1 Trait Writing	Web site that explains the 6+1 Trait Writing program from the Northwest Regional Educational Laboratory	www.nwrel.org/assessment/department.php?d=1
About.com	Environmental issues	www.environment.about.com
AltaVista	Search engine	www.altavista.com
Ask an Expert Page	Expert in any curricular area	www.askanexpert.com
Ask a Scientist	Scientific question and answer Web site	www.madsci.org/submit.html
Ask Dr. Universe	Students can ask questions about life, the universe, and other big ticket issues	www.wsu.edu/DrUniverse
Ask for Kids	Search engine	www.askforkids.com
Ask Wendell	Students can ask general questions and Wendell the worm makes sure they are answered	yucky.discovery.com/flash/askwendell/index.html
Association for Library Service to Children	Links to writing by children	www.ala.org/ala/alsc/greatwebsites/greatwebsiteswriting.htm
The Big6	An information and technology literacy model and curriculum	www.big6.com
The Blue Highway	Virtual field trip with a musical/rhythmic emphasis	www.thebluehighway.com
Blue Web'n	Rich teacher resource of Internet activities and projects	www.kn.pacbell.com/wired/bluewebn

(Continued)

(Continued)

Site Name	Comments	URL
Boiling Point of Water Example	Information exchange project activity	astro.uchicago.edu/cara/southpole.edu/boil.html
A Brief History of the Internet	Information regarding the origins of the Internet	www.isoc.org/internet/history/brief.shtml
The Bug Club	Virtual field trip with a naturalist emphasis	www.ex.ac.uk/bugclub
Building a Collaborative Web Project	Overview of designing Web projects	www.gsn.org/web/webproj/index.htm
Carl Hayden Bee Research Center	Virtual field trip with a naturalist emphasis	www.ars.usda.gov/Main/docs.htm?docid=12371
Children's Express	Web site created for electronic publishing of children's work	www.childrens-express.org
Children's Storybooks Online (K–3)	Virtual field trip with a verbal/linguistic emphasis	www.magickeys.com/books/index.html
Classics for Young People	Virtual field trip with a verbal/linguistic emphasis	www.ucalgary.ca/~dkbrown/storclas.html
Classroom Connect	Strong education site for teachers interested in using technology in the classroom	corporate.classroom.com
Comm Tech Lab	Learning exchange electronic publishing site	www.commtechlab.msu.edu/sites/letsnet/noframes/bigideas/b6/index.html
Describing Intelligences in Students	Includes a checklist for assessing students' multiple intelligences	www.ascd.org/ed_topics/2000armstrong/chapter3.html
Dogpile	Search engine	www.dogpile.com
Education Place (primary)	Comprehensive primary education site	www.eduplace.com
Educational Simulations	Teachers can explore educational simulations	www.simulations.com
Education World	Well-rounded education site	www.education-world.com
Electronic Emissary 1.0	Telementoring example	emissary.wm.edu
Electronic Reference Formats	Recommended by the American Psychological Association to help teachers and students reference electronic sources	www.apastyle.org/elecref.html
Envirolink	Lists of social action projects related to the environment	www.envirolink.org

Site Name	Comments	URL
Epals	Connect with classrooms from around the world or nation for keypal activities	www.epals.com
Essential Skills for Information Literacy	Information literacy skills	www.wlma.org/informationliteracy
Excite	Search engine	www.excite.com
Facing the Future	Social action Internet site	www.facingthefuture.org
Families and Friends	An information exchange activity relating to relationships with family and friends	www.kidlink.org/KIDFORUM/family
Field Guides Center	Excellent virtual field trip site offering numerous trips for students	www.field-guides.com
The First Seven and Then the Eighth	An interview with Howard Gardner regarding his addition of the naturalist intelligence	www.nea.org/teachexperience/braik030627.html
From Now On	An educational technology journal	www.fno.org
The Geometry Center	Virtual field trip with a logical/mathematical emphasis	www.geom.uiuc.edu
Get Active Stay Active	An activity log to monitor fitness	www.getactivestayactive.com
Global Grocery List Project	An information-gathering and analysis project where students share information on groceries and categorize information in a database	landmark-project.com/ggl
Global SchoolNet Foundation	A rich resource for K–12 teachers	www.globalschoolnet.org/index.html
Global SchoolNet's GeoGame	A geography game where students search for information to solve a geography question	www.gsn.org/GSH/project/gg
Green: Global Rivers Environmental Education Network	Social action projects and assistance related to water issues	www.earthforce.org/section/programs/green
Greenpeace.org	Greenpeace organization's updated information on what the organization is doing	www.greenpeace.org

(Continued)

(Continued)

Site Name	Comments	URL
Heinemann Interactive	Find keypals and register to meet other classes	www.hi.com.au
Historical Trees	An information exchange project based on sharing historical trees	www.nyu.edu/projects/julian/toc.html
HotBot	Search engine	www.hotbot.com
Hotlist of Virtual Field Trips	Resource for a variety of virtual field trip sites	www.kn.pacbell.com/wired/fil/pages/listvirtualgr.html
Hurricane: Storm Science Center	Virtual field trip with a naturalist emphasis	www.miamisci.org/hurricane
Intelligence in Seven Steps	Overview of multiple intelligences by Howard Gardner	www.newhorizons.org/future/Creating_the_Future/crfut_gardner.html
Intercultural E-Mail Classroom Connections	Find keypals from other countries	www.iecc.org
Internet4Classrooms Virtual Field Trips	Resource for a variety of virtual field trips	www.internet4classrooms.com/vft.htm
Internet Island	Visit to learn how to use the Internet in a classroom	www.miamisci.org/ii
In the Kitchen: Designs for Telecollaboration and Telepresence Introduction to Project-Based Learning	Judi Harris's site that provides links and ideas for the major Internet project type using projects in their curriculum	virtual-architecture.wm.edu/Telecollaboration/index.html
I Think . . . Therefore . . . MI	Extensive resources for and about the multiple intelligences with links to other relevant sites	www.surfaquarium.com/mi
Kathy Schrock's Guide for Educators	Excellent site with many resources	school.discovery.com/schrockguide/index.html
Kid Art	An information exchange project relating to kids' art	www.kidlink.org/KIDART
Kidlinks	An excellent Web site featuring a myriad of Internet activities with a focus on information exchange activities	www.kidlink.org
Kidlympics	Students report scores and times of physical education activities and participate in a pooled data analysis with other students	www.kidlink.org/KIDPROJ/Kidlympics

Site Name	Comments	URL
Kidnetic	Physical fitness resources and information exchange	www.kidnetic.com
KidPub	Writing and electronic publishing site for students	www.kidpub.com/kidpub
KidsBookshelf	Language arts site with homework help and writing resources	www.kidsbookshelf.com/gsfk/homeworkhelp.asp
Kids' Space	Writing and electronic publishing site for students	www.kids-space.org/story/story.html
Kidwriters Writing Studio	An information exchange activity related to student writing and electronic publishing	www.kidlink.org/KIDPROJ/Kidwriters
Learning Circles on iEARN	Provides teachers with an opportunity to join an interactive learning circle activity	www.iearn.org/circles
Learning Through Many Kinds of Intelligence	Dee Dickinson's overview of multiple intelligences	www.newhorizons.org/strategies/mi/dickinson_mi.html
Lightspan	Provides curriculum information, a large content base, and helpful links	www.lightspan.com
Mankato Schools Information Literacy Curriculum Guidelines	Information literacy skills	www.isd77.k12.mn.us/resources/infocurr/infolit.html
Martin Luther King Jr.	Virtual field trip with an interpersonal and intrapersonal emphasis	seattletimes.nwsource.com/mlk
Marvelous M&M Survey	Information-gathering and analysis project centered on having students work with M&M's	teams.lacoe.edu/documentation/projects/math/mm.html
The Math Forum	Math information and problems for students of all levels to solve in a possible parallel problem-solving activity	mathforum.org
MEGA Mathematics	A Web site dedicated to the exploration of mathematical concepts. Can be used as a virtual field trip.	www.c3.lanl.gov/mega-math
MidLink Magazine	E-zine dedicated to middle school students and providing an avenue for electronic publishing	mail.cs.ucf.edu/~MidLink

(Continued)

(Continued)

Site Name	Comments	URL
Multimedia and Multiple Intelligences	An article by Howard Gardner and Shirley Veenema	www.prospect.org/print/V7/29/veenema-s.html
Multiple Intelligences	Thomas Armstrong on Multiple Intelligences	www.thomasarmstrong.com/multiple_intelligences.htm
A Multiple Intelligences Bookshelf	Good links and resources for multiple intelligences	www.newhorizons.org/strategies/mi/front_mi.htm
Multiplying Intelligence in the Classroom	Bruce Campbell discusses his use of learning centers and multiple intelligences in an elementary classroom	www.newhorizons.org/strategies/mi/campbe113.htm
Music Pals	An information exchange project related to children's music	www.kidlink.org/KIDPROJ/Music
NASA: Virtual Conferences	Teleconference with NASA scientists	http://www.isoc.org/inet97/proceedings/A5/A5_2.HTM
National Budget Simulation	Simulation surrounding balancing the national budget	http://www.budgetsim.org/nbs
Negative Population Growth	Social action Internet site	www.npg.org
Nerds 2.0.1	History and workings of the Internet	www.pbs.org/opb/nerds2.0.1
Neuroscience for Kids	Virtual field trip opportunity relating to the brain	faculty.washington.edu/chudler/neurok.html
New Dimensions of Learning: Exploring Multiple Intelligences	Offers training and information relative to multiple intelligences	www.multi-intell.com
New York City Ballet	Virtual field trip with a bodily/kinesthetic emphasis	www.nycballet.com
Pow Wow Dancing	Virtual field trip with a bodily/kinesthetic emphasis	www.powwows.com
Project Zero	From Harvard University, where multiple intelligences theory began and continues	pzweb.harvard.edu
Questions Regarding the World Wide Web	Information about the World Wide Web	www.w3.0rg/People/Berners-Lee/FAQ.html
The Rivertown Simulation	Simulation including fictitious town undergoing revitalization; students make decisions regarding the revitalization process within a civic government setting	www.emich.edu/public/geo/rtownintro.html

Site Name	Comments	URL
Roald Dahl	Virtual field trip with a verbal/linguistic emphasis	www.roalddahlfans.com
Rock and Roll Hall of Fame	Virtual field trip with a musical/rhythmic emphasis	www.rockhall.com
Scholar Google	Search engine	www.scholar.google.com
Scholastic: Teachers	Resources for students, teachers, and parents that can be used in Internet activities	teacher.scholastic.com
Selected Civil War Photographs	Site dedicated to Civil War photographs that can be used in a virtual field trip activity	memory.loc.gov/ammem/cwphtml/cwphome.html
Sites for Teachers	Links to online publishing sites	www.sitesforteachers.com/resources_sharp/language_arts/la_pub.html
Teacher Magazine	Articles and current event topics in education	www.edweek.org
Teachers.Net Reference Desk	Lesson designs, references, and more	www.teachers.net/curriculum
TechLEARNING	E-zine covering technology in the classroom	www.techlearning.com
Telementoring	Site sponsored by the National Mentoring Partnership dedicated to linking telementors to students	www.telementoring.org
The United States Civil War Center	Civil War information that can be used in a virtual field trip activity	www.cwc.lsu.edu
The Valley of the Shadow	Civil War Web site that can be used for a virtual field trip activity	valley.vcdh.virginia.edu
Virtual Fieldtrips	Lists of field trip opportunities	www.geocities.com/CollegePark/Union/2106/fieldtrip.htm
The WebQuest Page	Active student inquiry projects that can be used in information search activities	webquest.sdsu.edu
WhaleNet	Virtual field trip with a naturalist emphasis	whale.wheelock.edu/Welcome.html

(Continued)

(Continued)

Site Name	Comments	URL
What's My Number?	An information exchange site focused on math	kidspace.kidlink.org/kidspace/start .cfm?HoldNode=899
Women of NASA	Provides students with electronic appearances and personal profiles of woman scientists	quest.arc.nasa.gov/women/intro.html
Writer's Corner Café!	Site dedicated to helping writers as well as provide an opportunity for sequential creation activities	www.mv.com/Writers-Corner/Homepage.html
Writing.Com	New England Writing Group Web page	www.writing.com/?rfrc=inkspot.com
Yahoo!	Search engine	www.yahoo.com
Yahoo! Kids	Search engine for children	http://kids.yahoo.com/
The Young Writers Club	For children who enjoy writing and want to be electronically published as well as receive peer feedback	www.cs.bilkent.edu.tr/~david/derya/ywc.html
ZuZu	A site where students can share writings and accompanying artwork	www.zuzu.org

Appendix B

Rubrics

Web Site Evaluation Form

Web site: ______________________ Score: ______________________

Score: 1 = *Does not meet criterion;* 2 = *Meets criterion adequately;* 3 = *Meets criterion very well*

Evaluation Criteria	Rubric Score	Comments
1. Does the Web site help teachers meet the standards or understanding goals?	1 2 3	
2. Does the Web site allow for two-way interaction?	1 2 3	
3. Is the Web site visually appealing?	1 2 3	
4. Is the Web site easy to navigate?	1 2 3	
5. Is the Web site fast loading?	1 2 3	
6. Does the Web site allow students to publish their work or to display some final outcome?	1 2 3	
7. Does the Web site activate more than one of the multiple intelligences?	1 2 3	
8. Is the information on the Web site verifiable? Is the information reliable and consistent? Is the material fact or opinion without substantiation?	1 2 3	
9. Is the Web site consistent with current brain-based teaching concepts?	1 2 3	
10. Does the Web site meet the standard or understanding goal or could the standard or goal be met better using some other medium?	1 2 3	
11. How recent is the information or research on the Web site?	1 2 3	

Understanding Assessment Form

Student Name: ______________________ Score: ______________________

Assessment for: ______________________ Grade: ______________________

1 = Does not display ability in work to 5 = Displays ability throughout work showing an understanding of concepts and ideas.

Facet of Understanding	Explanation of Understanding	Assessment Rubric and Comments
Explanation	• An ability to explain ideas and concepts using knowledgeable accounts of events and ideas	1 2 3 4 5 Comments:
Interpretation	• An ability to make an interpretation of events and ideas • Describe an event's significance and importance	1 2 3 4 5 Comments:
Application	• An ability to use knowledge effectively in new and diverse situations (i.e., the ability to use the information and understanding in new ways)	1 2 3 4 5 Comments:
Perspective	• An ability to form critical and insightful points of view • Perceive things from an objective point of view • Recognize that multiple perspectives exist for any complex issue	1 2 3 4 5 Comments:
Empathy	• The ability to understand another person's feelings and perceptions • To walk in another's shoes • To grasp another's emotional reactions and reality	1 2 3 4 5 Comments:
Self-Knowledge	• The ability to recognize what one knows and does not know and how one's patterns of thought and action inform as well as hinder understanding	1 2 3 4 5 Comments:

Understanding Rubric

Student Name: ______________________ Score: ______________________

Rubric for: ______________________ Grade: ______________________

Facet of Understanding	Masterful (3)	Skilled (2)	Basic (1)
Explanation			
Interpretation			
Application			
Perspective			
Empathy			
Self-Knowledge			
Internet Skills			
Use of Multiple Intelligences			

Information Literacy Skills Rubric

Student Name: ______________________ Score: ______________________

Rubric for: ______________________ Grade: ______________________

Information Literacy Skill	Masterful (3)	Skilled (2)	Basic (1)
1. Know when there is a need for information. (Comprehension)			
2. Find and identify the information needed. (Comprehension and Analysis)			
3. Analyze the information. (Analysis and Evaluation)			
4. Organize the information. (Application)			
5. Use the information effectively to address the problem or task. (Synthesis)			
6. Communicate the information and evaluate the results. (Application and Evaluation)			

Generalized Multiple Intelligences Rubric

Student Name: ______________________ Score: ______________________

Rubric for: ______________________ Grade: ______________________

Intelligence	Masterful (3)	Skilled (2)	Basic (1)
Verbal/Linguistic			
Logical/Mathematical			
Visual/Spatial			
Musical/Rhythmic			
Bodily/Kinesthetic			
Interpersonal			
Intrapersonal			
Naturalist			

Internet Skills Rubric

Student Name: ______________________ Score: ______________________

Rubric for: ______________________ Grade: ______________________

Internet Skill	Masterful (3)	Skilled (2)	Basic (1)
Search Engines			
E-Mail			
Bookmarks and Folders			
Links			
Internet Technology			
Download Files			
E-Mail Etiquette			
Web Site Evaluation			

Notes

Chapter 2

1. Ideas from Caine, R. and Caine, G. are reprinted by permission, *Making Connections: Teaching and the Human Brain,* by Caine, R. and Caine, G. Alexandria, VA: ASCD, 1991. The Association for Supervision and Curriculum Development is a worldwide community of educators advocating sound policies and sharing best practices to achieve the success of each learner. To learn more, visit ASCD at www.ascd.org

2. Ideas from S. Kovalik & Associates are used with permission, *Exceeding Expectations: A User's Guide to Implementing Brain Research in the Classroom,* by Kovalik, S. and Olsen, K., 2002.

3. David Sousa's ideas are used with permission, *How the Brain Learns, 3rd Edition,* David A. Sousa; Corwin Press, © 2006.

4. Ideas from Sylwester, R. are reprinted by permission, *A Celebrating of Neurons: An Educator's Guide to the Human Brain,* by Sylwester, R. Alexandria, VA: ASCD, 1995. The Association for Supervision and Curriculum Development is a worldwide community of educators advocating sound policies and sharing best practices to achieve the success of each learner. To learn more, visit ASCD at www.ascd.org

Introduction and Chapters 3, 4, 5, and 6

5. Judi Harris's items and ideas are adapted and reprinted with permission from Judi Harris, *Virtual Architecture: Designing and Directing Curriculum-Based Telecomputing,* © 1998 Judi Harris. All rights reserved.

6. Ideas from H. Wenglinsky are reprinted by permission, *Technology and Achievement: The Bottom Line, from Educational Leadership (63) 4, p. 30,* by Wenglinsky, H. Alexandria,VA: ASCD, December 2005/January 2006. The Association for Supervision and Curriculum Development is a worldwide community of educators advocating sound policies and sharing best practices to achieve the success of each learner. To learn more, visit ASCD at www.ascd.org

7. The Understanding by Design framework is adapted with permission from *Understanding by Design* by Wiggins, Grant and McTighe, Jay. Alexandria, VA: ASCD, 1998, pp 9–10, 14–16, 27, 31, 76–77. The Association for Supervision and Curriculum Development is a worldwide community of educators advocating sound policies and sharing best practices to achieve the success of each learner. To learn more, visit ASCD at www.ascd.org

Chapter 3

8. Robert Marzano's ideas are reprinted by permission, *What Works in Schools: Translating Research Into Action*, by Marzano, Robert J. Alexandria, VA: ASCD, 2003, p. 112. The Association for Supervision and Curriculum Development is a worldwide community of educators advocating sound policies and sharing best practices to achieve the success of each learner. To learn more, visit ASCD at www.ascd.org

Chapter 5

9. 6+1 Trait materials are copyrighted and trademarked by the Northwest Regional Educational Laboratory, "6+1 Traits of Writing Rubrics and Definitions." Retrieved December 7, 2006, from http://www.nwrel.org/assessment/department.php?d=1. Reprinted with permission.

Chapter 6

10. Mary Burns's ideas are reprinted by permission, *Tools for the Mind*, by Burns, Mary. Alexandria, VA: ASCD, 2006. The Association for Supervision and Curriculum Development is a worldwide community of educators advocating sound policies and sharing best practices to achieve the success of each learner. To learn more, visit ASCD at www.ascd.org

Bibliography

Armstrong, T. (1987). *In their own way: Discovering and encouraging your child's personal learning style*. Los Angeles: Jeremy P. Tarcher.

Armstrong, T. (1991). *Awakening your child's natural genius: Enhancing curiosity, creativity, and learning ability*. New York: Putnam.

Armstrong, T. (1994). *Multiple intelligences in the classroom*. Alexandria, VA: Association for Supervision and Curriculum Development.

Bellanca, J., Chapman, C., & Swartz, B. (1994). *Multiple assessments for multiple intelligences*. Thousand Oaks, CA: Corwin Press.

Bloom, B. (1956). *Taxonomy of educational objectives*. New York: David McKay.

Bruetsch, A. (1995). *Multiple intelligences lesson plan book*. Tucson, AZ: Zephyr.

Burns, M. (2006). *Tools for the mind. Education Leadership, 63*(4), 48–53.

Caine, R., & Caine, G. (1991). *Making connections: Teaching and the human brain*. Alexandria, VA: Association for Supervision and Curriculum Development.

Campbell, B. (1994). *The multiple intelligences handbook: Lesson plans and more*. Stanwood, WA: Author.

Campbell, B., & Campbell, L. (1999). *Multiple intelligences and student achievement: Success stories from six schools*. Alexandria, VA: Association for Supervision and Curriculum Development.

Campbell, L., Campbell, B., & Dickinson, D. (1992). *Teaching and learning through multiple intelligences*. Seattle, WA: New Horizons for Learning.

Carbo, M. (1986). *Teaching students to read through their individual learning styles*. Englewood Cliffs, NJ: Prentice-Hall.

Cooper, G., & Cooper, G. (1997). *Virtual field trips*. Littleton, CO: Libraries Unlimited.

Csikszentmihalyi, M. (1990). *Flow: The psychology of optimal experience*. New York: Harper & Row.

Culham, R., & Spandel, V. (1995). *Writing from the inside out: Revising for quality*. Portland, OR: Northwest Regional Education Laboratory.

Eisenberg, M. B., & Berkowitz, R. E. (1992). Information problem solving: The big six skills approach. *School Library Media Activities Monthly, 8*(5):27–29, 37, 42.

Eisenberg, M. B., & Johnson, D. (1996). *Computer skills for information problem solving: Learning and teaching technology in context*. Syracuse, NY: ERIC Clearinghouse on Information and Technology. (ERIC Document Reproduction Service No. ED392463)

Faculty of the New City School. (1994). *Celebrating multiple intelligences: Teaching for success*. St. Louis, MO: The New City School.

Fogarty, R. (1993). *Integrating the curricula: A collection*. Thousand Oaks, CA: Corwin Press.

Fogarty, R. (1995). *Multiple intelligences: A collection*. Thousand Oaks, CA: Corwin Press.

Fogarty, R. (1997). *Problem-based learning and other curriculum models for the multiple intelligences classroom*. Thousand Oaks, CA: Corwin Press.

Fogarty, R. (2001). *Brain-compatible classrooms* (2nd ed.). Thousand Oaks, CA: Corwin Press.

Gardner, H. (1983). *Frames of mind: The theory of multiple intelligences*. New York: Basic.

Gardner, H. (1991). *The unschooled mind: How children think and how schools should teach*. New York: Basic.

Gardner, H. (2006). *Multiple intelligences: The theory in practice*. New York: New Horizons.

Goleman, D. (1995). *Emotional intelligence*. New York: Bantam Books.

Harris, J. (1998). *Virtual architecture: Designing and directing curriculum-based telecomputing*. Eugene, OR: International Society for Technology in Education Publications.

Hart, L. A. (1983). *Human brain, human learning*. Kent, WA: Books for Educators.

Healy, J. (1990). *Endangered minds: Why children don't think and what we can do about it*. New York: Doubleday.

Heidi, A., & Stilborne, L. (1996). *The teacher's complete and easy guide to the Internet*. Ontario, Canada: Trifolium Books.

Hoff, D. J. (1999, September). Digital content and the curriculum. *Technology counts '99: Building the digital curriculum. Education Week, 19*(4), 51–60.

James, J. (1996). *Thinking in the future tense: Leadership skills for a new age*. New York: Simon & Schuster.

Kovalik, S., & Olsen, K. (2002). *Exceeding expectations: A user's guide to implementing brain research in the classroom*. Covington, WA: Susan Kovalik & Associates.

Lazear, D. (1991). *Seven ways of teaching: The artistry of teaching with multiple intelligences*. Thousand Oaks, CA: Corwin Press.

Lazear, D. (1994). *Multiple intelligences approaches to assessment*. Tucson, AZ: Zephyr.

Lazear, D. (1998). *The rubrics way: Using MI to assess understanding*. Tucson, AZ: Zephyr.

LeDoux, J. E. (1996). *The emotional brain*. New York: Simon & Schuster.

Lenaghan, D. D. (1998). Internet for the intellects. Retrieved December 7, 2006 from http://www.multigogy.com/learning/internet.htm

Levine, J., Baroudi, C., & Young, M. L. (1998). *The Internet for dummies*. Chicago: International Data Group Books.

McLain, T. (1999). *How to create successful Internet projects*. El Segundo, CA: Classroom Connect.

Marzano, R. (2003). *What works in schools: Translating research into action*. Alexandria, VA: Association of Supervision and Curriculum Development.

Northwest Regional Educational Laboratory. (2000). 6+1 traits of writing rubrics and definitions. Retrieved December 7, 2006, from http://www.nwrel.org/assessment/department.php?d=1

Sapolsky, R. (1994). *Why zebras don't get ulcers*. New York: W. H. Freeman.

Schlechty, P. (1990). *Schools for the 21st century*. San Francisco: Jossey-Bass.

Schmoker, M. (1999). *Results: The key to continuous school improvement*. Alexandria, VA: Association of Supervision and Curriculum Development.

Sousa, D. (2006). *How the brain learns* (3rd ed.). Thousand Oaks, CA: Corwin Press.

Sylwester, R. (1995). *A celebration of neurons: An educator's guide to the human brain*. Alexandria, VA: Association of Supervision and Curriculum Development.

Treadwell, M. (1999). *1001 of the best Internet sites for educators*. Thousand Oaks, CA: Corwin Press.

Wenglinsky, H. (2006). Technology and achievement: The bottom line. *Education Leadership, 63*(4), 29–32.

Wiggins, G., & McTighe, J. (2005). *Understanding by design*. Alexandria, VA: Association for Supervision and Curriculum Development. (Original work published 1998).

Wiske, S. (1998). *Teaching for understanding with technology part 1*. Paper presented at Leadership and the New Technologies Summer Institute Workshop, Harvard University, Cambridge, MA.

Wolfe, P. (2001). *Brain matters: Translating research into classroom practice*. Alexandria, VA: Association for Supervision and Curriculum Development.

Index